# THE MORBID CURIOUS

*Magic, Mystery & Murder Issue!*

The

# MORBID CURIOUS

NO. 12

*The Journal of Ghosts, Murder & the Macabre*

# MORBID CURIOUS NO. 12

© Copyright 2025 by Troy Taylor

All Rights Reserved.

Published by American Hauntings Ink

301 East Broadway – Alton, IL – 62oo2

www.americanhauntingsink.com

Cover Design by April Slaughter

Editor and Interior Design by Troy Taylor

Contact: ghosts@americanhauntings.net

First Edition – October 2025
ISBN: 978-1-958589-28-1

Printed in the United States of America

# TABLE OF CONTENTS

# The Magic of Adelaide Herrmann

# SLEIGHT OF HAND & TWIST OF FATE

# SUSAN A. JACOBUCCI

A middle-aged woman felt faint as she tentatively stepped on stage to the Strauss waltz. Her wavy auburn hair upswept; she dressed in dark knee breeches and a white billowy shirt, an outfit like one her husband once wore. The woman took centerstage at the Metropolitan Opera House in New York during the evening of January 28, 1897. The crowd grew hushed right before the sound of a gunshot reverberated throughout the performance hall. Who was this woman who stood in the path of a bullet intending to catch it with her bare hands? How did she get into this predicament where her whole career and livelihood depended on the successful execution of this death-defying stunt, an illusion she was aware had a "sanguinary record?" The woman was none other than Adelaide Herrmann, the "Queen of Magic."

The late nineteenth through early twentieth centuries was a period known as "The Golden Age of Magic." Magicians centered within extravagant theatrical performances were commonplace on Broadway, music and town halls, public gardens, museums, and entertainment venues around the world. Many of these predominately male magicians initially achieved widespread notoriety and financial success in Europe before taking their shows on the road to America. Alexander Herrmann, also known as Herrmann the Great, born in 1844 in France into a family of illusionists was one such renowned conjurer of the late nineteenth century. Herrmann resembled the romanticized representation of a magician, "a man with thick, wavy hair, wearing a top hat, sporting a goatee, and dressed in a tailcoat" as described by the American Museum of Magic. It was Herrmann's captivating presence and magnificent performance that mesmerized his future wife, Adelaide, at Egyptian Hall, in London and was the impetus in her transformation into one of the greatest female magicians of all time.

Adelaide's husband, the famous magician, Alexander Herrmann, who was billed as "Herrmann the Great"

*Adelaide Scarsez, who later became Adelaide Herrmann*

Adelaide was born Adele Scarsez on August 11, 1853, in London, England. According to her memoir edited by Margaret Steele and published in 2012, as a child Adelaide was fascinated by stage performances; she looked forward to pantomime season and was excited whenever the circus came to town. The first time Adelaide attended a ballet, the dancers instantaneously captivated her. One day Adelaide answered a newspaper advertisement and joined a dance academy, run by the Kiralfys, a family of Hungarian dancers. In time, Adelaide's

hard work and dedication to the craft paid off. The Kiralfys welcomed her into their dance troupe for an initial engagement in New York City, which transformed into a United States tour. When Adelaide's contract ended, she and three other girls from the troupe were engaged to perform at the once prestigious Howard Athenaeum in Boston, Massachusetts, demolished in 1962 after a fire. While performing in Boston, love bloomed. Adelaide developed a romantic relationship with Gus Williams, an American comedian and songwriter. The two became engaged; however, their relationship fizzled after Adelaide returned to Europe. She wrote about the break-up, "fate had other designs for me."

Adelaide not only attended Alexander Herrmann's performance at Egyptian Hall, but she was part of his act. When the great magician asked the audience for a lady volunteer to give him a ring, without hesitation, Adelaide gave him her engagement ring which he proceeded to burn on stage only to return it to her "on a ribbon tied around the neck of a beautiful white dove." After the performance, the two met backstage for pleasantries. Their paths would cross once again in the future. Adelaide would first learn to expertly ride a velocipede, a precursor to today's bicycle; join a company of lady riders who performed throughout France before they set sail for an American tour. During the voyage, their steamship stopped at Queenstown, Ireland to pick up passengers. Adelaide described one of the new passengers who boarded the ship as "tall, handsome and distinguished-looking man enveloped in a luxurious fur coat." As fate would have it, Alexander Herrmann was the passenger. He traveled to the United States to go on a tour arranged coincidentally by the same manager who organized Adelaide's velocipede commitment. During the two-week voyage Adelaide spent a good deal of time with Alexander and shortly thereafter the two were engaged and later married on March 27, 1875.

They toured independently with their own show once their contractual agreements were complete. Through hard work and perseverance, it took a while for their act to establish a foothold even though their performances always gained glorious press reviews. Initially Adelaide wrote their show consisted of "eighteen sleight-of-hand tricks but no illusions, the performance being, divided into two parts, nine tricks in each." Alexander performed his prestidigitation up close and personal with his audience where his charismatic and hypnotic presence shone. Originally Adelaide's role was to obtain objects from the audience for Alexander to manipulate. She was his principal assistant, but soon began performing some of the tricks, billed as Mr. Alexander and dressed as a man.

The couple worked endlessly creating original content for their shows and they were the first to present as Adelaide described, "magic in spectacular form, thus revolutionizing public presentation of the magic art." Upon Adelaide's suggestion, they introduced stunning illusions, complete with extraordinarily intricately painted scenery with full orchestras performing unique scores for each trick. Adelaide played the part of a medium in one such illusion, "duplicating all the familiar spiritualistic manifestations presented by professional mediums" and in another ghostly act called "Dark Séance" that produced seemingly real supernatural spirits and skeletons that left audiences mystified and reeling for more. They also included death defying stunts such as "The Bullet-Catching Trick" and "The Cannon Act" which featured Adelaide, referred to as Mademoiselle Addie shot from a cannon. Over time Adelaide incorporated velocipede routines and dances into their performances, including her rendition of the Serpentine Dance, popular in the late eighteen hundreds, which featured the dancer wearing a draping dress made of yards of silk she would manipulate into varying forms.

The Herrmanns toured North and South America and Europe, including travels on horseback to isolated locations in mountainous regions. On one such trip to a remote area of Mexico they purchased birds, snakes, and monkeys from locals with many of these animals incorporated into their illusions, while they kept several as cherished pet companions. They were generous, championed many causes, oftentimes donating their time and travel expenses to perform for poverty stricken or to raise money for those in need. They lived a rich lifestyle, commonly spent everything they earned on lavish parties, leased expensive real estate such as Whitestone Manor, their estate retreat on Long Island Sound, leased and rehabbed theaters, purchased rare antiques, regal jewelry, and lavish clothing, while many of their hosts doted on them with priceless gifts. Alexander purchased his own ornate railcar that included their bedrooms, a guest room, kitchen, storage rooms, servant's quarters, and space for their animals, enough space to transport their traveling menagerie.

Alexander smoked and suffered from minor heart attacks for some time, which did not stop the couple from traveling, performing, and living a large life. It was December 14, 1896, when they and their entourage arrived in Rochester, New York to visit and perform for boys attending the State Industrial School. Following the performance, they hooked their car back onto a train, and headed to Bradford, Pennsylvania. While on route, Adelaide was washing her hair when she heard Alexander throw himself on her bed. She glanced towards him and immediately noticed his ashen face, his eyes stared straight ahead. Adelaide rushed to his side and helped him to his room. Alexander took a glass of warm water and bicarbonate from his valet's hand, gulped down a sip of the mixture and instantly disappeared from the ranks of the living.

Stunned and in shock, Adelaide writes, "I hardly knew which way to turn." Throngs of people from all levels of society attended her husband's funeral; the wealthy, the famous, and his servants among others were in attendance. The press idolized him, but Adelaide had no time to morn. She writes, "hearts may be torn, bitter tears may be shed, but we on stage have a jealous mistress in the public, which demands that we be gnawing at the soul." Once Adelaide settled Alexander's affairs, his estate was worth less than two thousand dollars as reported in an edition of the New York Times, published December 22, 1896, referenced by Margaret Steele. Adelaide received an offer to purchase their magic entourage which she declined. An 1896 edition of the New Jersey Mirror quoted Adelaide as saying, "I am trying my best to bear up under my affliction, as it is my duty to continue the tour in order to act honorably by his creditors."

Adelaide found herself with her back against the wall. She had no choice but to perform not only out of financial necessity, but to honor her husband's legendary stature, and to satisfy her own desire to perform. Adelaide respected her husband's wishes to have his nephew Leon in Paris succeed him. She sent for Leon who strikingly resembled a younger version of Alexander. After intensive rehearsals, they were ready for their first show in which they would perform her husband's tricks on January 10, 1897, at Hoyt's Theater near Madison Square Garden. Adelaide and Leon were Alexander's worthy successors. Their debut was a smashing success; however, they were in a financial hole for their next show. Adelaide knew she needed to do something to create an audience feeding frenzy to sell out their upcoming performance on January 28, 1897. She announced she would perform her husband's death-defying illusion, the "Bullet-Catching Trick."

Adelaide wrote about her "deep-rooted aversion to the trick," she deemed dangerous. She was intimate with the history of performances that proved fatal. She described several perilous occurrences that resulted either out of sheer accident, one magician's desire to commit suicide onstage, or of a malcontent who "slyly dropped a few slugs into the pistol, with the result that the

*Illustration of Adelaide Printed in the Virginian-Pilot newspaper*

conjuror was frightfully wounded." Because of the death-defying quality of the illusion, her husband had only performed it sparingly. Adelaide could not let her nerves be a dooming factor. She stepped onstage, cleared her mind of all thoughts and sounds, and expertly performed the trick at the Metropolitan

*Adelaide Herrmann – Library of Congress*

Opera House. Afterward she wrote, "the idea of a woman doing this dangerous trick created an even greater sensation than its presentation by my husband."

The newly formed ensemble, Herrmann the Great Company, organized by Adelaide took their act on the road. Glorious reviews described their performances; however, after three seasons Adelaide and Leon parted ways. Adelaide explained they did so until she was certain "he was capable of carrying on alone." Reports published in the New York Tribune, February 2, 1902, and March 18, 1907, editions suggest their breakup was not amicable; Leon wanted to tour on his own. Nevertheless, the two went their separate ways. Leon initially performed on

Vaudeville but returned to Europe where he had a rough go of it, which ended in his unexpected death in 1909.

Adelaide's Whitestone estate proved to be too large for her needs. She moved out of the home and rented an apartment in New York City. She downsized her possessions, kept her favorites, and auctioned off the rest. She lived a simpler life, spending most of her time excelling in her craft. The press considered her to be the "only woman wizard in the world." Adelaide played jam packed audiences and traveled the world. Her performances matched and exceeded her male counterparts because she presented intricately planned, multidisciplined presentations consisting of all aspects of magic from close-up sleight of hand to dangerous life defying stunts and included culturally artistic dance routines. She introduced grandiose, and breathtaking acts that she and her departed husband had only envisioned. In one such act, "Noah's Ark," which Adelaide refurbished from one of her husband's short-lived attractions, she produced an empty remodeled ark onstage. Out of nowhere water poured down a chimney with an ensuing procession of exotic and domestic animals including lions, tigers, and elephants, among other creatures appearing, marching two by two down a gangplank.

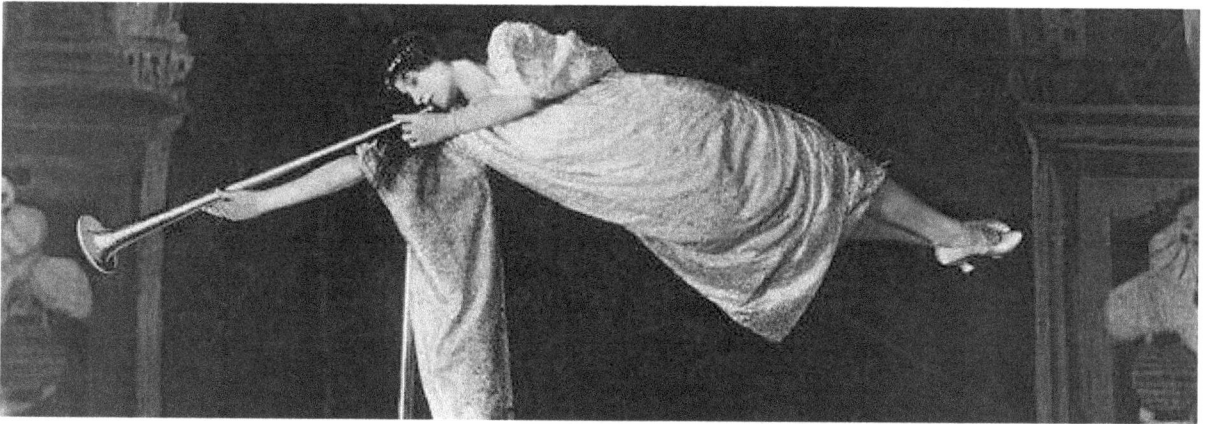

Adelaide housed her illusions and trained animals at a rented loft on Thirty-Seventh Street, New York. During the summer of 1926 she worked tiredly building and rebuilding her illusions, getting them ready for her season opener on September 10th in Chicago. On September 7th, a terrible explosion left her loft engulfed in flames. Adelaide rushed to the scene to find out that most of her trained animals perished in the fire except Magic, her white cat who leaped from the fourth floor upon hearing Adelaide's voice and two dogs from her Noah's Ark illusion. An explosion of alcohol stills kept on the top floor of the building caused the fire and claimed the life of Thomas Collins, a veteran animal trainer, injured two other animal trainers, and killed over two hundred animals. Fire and water destroyed all of Adelaide's illusions. She writes, "summoning all my remaining courage to my aid, I clung persistently to the thought that I should again arise, phoenix-like from these ashes to face another future."

Adelaide did indeed rise above this tragedy; she continued to perform on a simpler scale until she was seventy-nine years old. An illness that developed into pneumonia extinguished the Queen of Magic's life on February 19, 1932.

She described herself as a "gambler at heart" and "one of the most indefatigable workers on the stage...striving for new effects-adding a new shade here and a novel musical change there." Adelaide's desire for experimentation, perfection, sheer passion, and her survivalist skills propelled her from one stage of life to another. After Alexander's death she returned to the stage for several reasons. And perhaps also because executing magic made her feel close to her departed husband; however, Adelaide had a propensity to perform, to perform magic, and she excelled at it. She reached out to Leon for assistance because of her husband's wishes but also due to the time in which she lived, it was commonplace for women to have men assist them. She initially relied on Leon to fulfill the performing role that her husband had vacated, but she soon learned she did not need him at all.

Adelaide was talented in her craft. She became a top act and world renowned. With synchronized, rote hand movements and illustrious set designs she held her audience hostage to their seats, demanding more. Adelaide's generosity, her talent and drive, and most of all her survival skills, endeared her to me. When I discovered she had written a memoir about her life published posthumously by Margaret Steele, I akin to her audience, anchored myself to my seat, and demanded to learn more about her. It was difficult to find a copy of the out-of-print memoir; however, I seemingly tracked down a print offered for sale on an online rare book dealer website. I paid for expedited shipping and when I received my package; ripped it open and held a book in my hands titled, "Magic Tales: Told-Again Tales From Many Lands" written by Adelaide Holl.

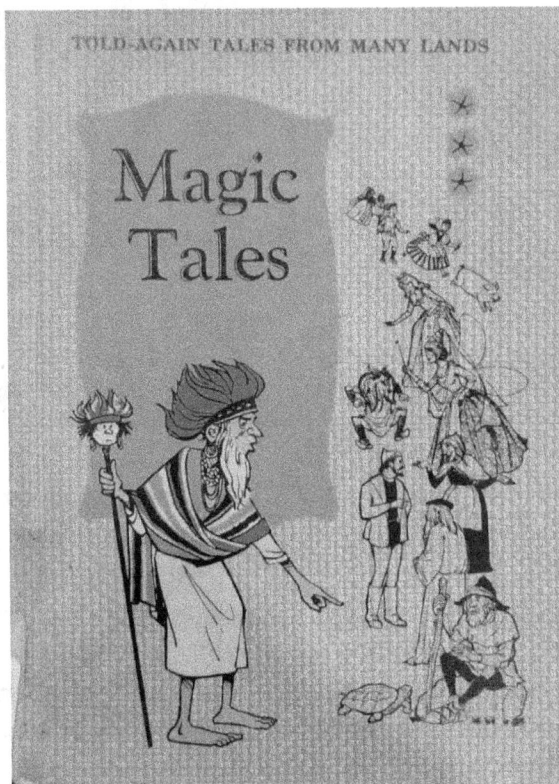

*Photograph by Nathan Thompson*

I felt perplexed and stared at the book for a while and thought perhaps Adelaide also wrote under a pen name. It took a while for it to sink in; the rare book company performed a sleight of hand illusion in front of me; and poof, a children's book about magic tales from around the world materialized. Adelaide Holl and Adelaide Herrmann have nothing in common except for their first names, last names began with the letter "H," and they both wrote about magic. I decided to keep Holl's book and continued my search through various rare publication websites until I was able to find a copy of Adelaide's memoir which I will forever cherish.

Adelaide Herrmann is as illusive in death as she was in life. She had the ability to convince her audience to believe she was who they thought she was, a wonder-worker who performed with strength, grace, beauty, and at times narrowly escaped dangerous situations only to rise like a phoenix out of the flaming ashes of despair to perform another day.

# VICTORIA JAYE

# UNHOLY POWER & THIRD ACT MADNESS

## The Witches' Sabbat in Film

*The Witches' Sabbat by Francisco de Goya*

## Introduction

As an enjoyer of witch-related media, I have noticed that the third act of several witch movies feature an extremely wild sabbat that ends in blood, mania, mayhem, and more blood. I'll be analyzing *Lords of Salem* (2012), *The Witch* (2015), and *Suspiria* (2018) as film depictions of Witches' Sabbat rituals; specifically, I'll be examining how one never really knows what's going to happen in the third act, but that the imagery will likely not leave in a hurry. I will be using the terms "Sabbath" and "Sabbat" interchangeably since there seems to be no actual difference between the two.

## Witch *Folkloresque*

*Folkloresque* is a term from folklore studies used to describe stories and media that is either built on real folklore that has new, invented elements or a story that feels like folklore but isn't. Many of these movies play into the historical imagery of what people mistakenly believe is witch folklore of the early modern era, from 1450-1800. The problem is that this 'folklore' isn't based on anything but overblown fantasies of clergymen who were worried about things they *imagined* witches were up to instead of what they were actually doing[i]. Examples of this type of fantasy were witch familiars, or demons disguised as animals – which accompanied the appearance of a witches' teat where those familiars suck, which wouldn't bleed if pricked. This is one of the tests conducted on accused witches if a mole or birthmark was found on them. Witches were also popularly thought to be using demons to carry out their misdeeds, fornicating with the devil, dancing naked around fires while covered in blood, and hurting the innocent. This same demonizing process also happened during the 1980s with Satanic Panic, a moral panic, when an entire group of people becomes feared and hated—instead of witches being blamed in that case, it was Satanists.

"Witch" became a catch-all term for anyone dealing in perceived magical means of medicine or fortune-telling. Julio Caro Baroja cautions the reader that, "probably 2/3 of the material collected about witches were the anxieties of the teller than the reality of tradition". Clergymen were likely worried about the consolidation of their own power against these 'witches' that were actually cunning folk or healers; these were knowledgeable people that helped others where the church either could not or did not. They operated in the open and were needed in village culture to solve everyday ailments; magic workers were largely tolerated by those in power until they weren't.

Anne Llewellyn Barstow noted that women were four times as likely to be accused of witchery than men because the persecutions were a response to growing social power that their talents gave them in communities. Occultism eventually became "politically threatening to institutions", which forced a woman's place in society to be redefined for submission to male authority. Men, however, were accused and murdered as well. The creation of documents like the *Malleus Malificarum*, a manual on how to find and kill witches led to the hunting down and execution of the magically skilled.

## The Sabbat Historically

The term "sabbat" likely comes from the Hebrew word that means "day of rest", though it is not known for sure. Christians adopted this concept into one day (Sunday) that's much shorter than it is in Judaism. A Sabbat for witches was thought to be a mockery of the Lord's Sabbath; it also connected the antisemitic and fear-based dots between Jews and witches for medieval Christians.

These sabbats emerged in witch-related narratives of the fifteenth century where witches would gather to renew their allegiance to Satan (with other demons in attendance) in exchange for unholy powers, celebrating Satan's glory, and partaking in hedonistic sexual activity. There's no real evidence these types of sensational assemblies of blasphemous witches worshipping the Devil ever happened. That's not to say small covens never met during an event, but it was not the shocking gathering that clergymen imagined it to be.

The term "witches sabbath" didn't show up until 1613 in print with Francis Brooke's translation of Vincent Le Blanc's book, *The World Surveyed;* this was the first time it referred to sorcery at all. French and Francophone authors (writing in Latin) used this term much more than other writers of the time, but still somewhat rarely. Even 150 years later during the witch panics and subsequent persecutions of magical people, it mainly was the Francophone writers using such terms though again, not as much as one would expect. The term "witches' sabbath" also shows up in translations of fine art from Hans Baldung, Frans Francken, Jacob van Swanenburg, Francisco Goya, and Luis Ricardo Falero, pieces that spanned from 1510 to 1880.

Scott E. Hendrix gives us an explanation of why these stories were so pervasive even though there isn't a shred of truth to them: the belief in witches' powers were on the rise, which fueled the paranoia of the religiously powerful. They imagined the existence of a vast witch conspiracy network to overthrow them and Christianity in general. Women that were seen as no longer useful to communities (so past child-bearing years) were an easy scapegoat for anything that could go wrong in a community; they also were a significant drain on shared resources, so many jumped on the bandwagon to get rid of these so-called "witches." The lurid details of witch folkloresque were then relayed to many others, growing and changing with each retelling but told as pure fact.

Ronald Hutton tells us that the idea of a witches' sabbath is a more modern construction because of its mythical components from older traditions, which included:

"(1) A procession of female spirits, often joined by privileged human beings and often led by a supernatural woman;

(2) A lone spectral huntsman, regarded as demonic, accursed, or otherworldly;

(3) A procession of the human dead, normally thought to be wandering to expiate their sins, often noisy and tumultuous, and usually consisting of those who had died prematurely and violently"

The first part is pre-Christian in its origins and likely directly influenced the concept formation of the witches' sabbath. The other two appear to be a medieval creation but the third is directly related to people wondering about what happens to the dead during the 11th and 12th centuries. A mishmash of older tradition with more modern, invented details is often how folklore develops over time.

## The Unseen, Salacious Sabbat

In the 1608 book, *Compendium Maleficarum* by Francesco Maria Guazzo, we are given details of witch-related folk beliefs (or common beliefs of the culture) from the time. Goats would be ridden to the Sabbat where the cross would be trampled, a re-baptism in the Devil's name done, ones' clothes given to Satan, kissing his rear end, and dancing in a circle. Other named "diabolical elements" were the eating of babies (or using their fat as part of a flying ointment), the poisoning of wells, and the desecration of hosts--

maligned groups such as heretic Christians, lepers, Muslims, and Jews were also accused of such acts.

Such descriptions of Sabbats were interesting because it was pure imagination: they were created by priests, juries, judges, and religious authorities who never took part in nor saw such gatherings. Details were also extracted from the confessions that were tortured out of people who would say anything to make their physical pain stop. Such narratives only reflect the anxieties of the time along with fear, ignorance, and intolerance.

The sabbat functioned almost as an advertisement to propagate fear of the witches and faith in communities but ended in the systematic extermination of alleged witches that were likely not up to witchery at all.

The public was dually fascinated by and reviled by witches' supposed activities. Likely this had to do with hedonistic imaginings the likes of which repressed societies could scarcely dream of, but they definitely heard about. Perverse sexuality with Satan, demons, beasts, and human orgies were common narrative factors; it kept shocked Christians in line and kept people sterile in these narratives, which could then be blamed for sudden crop failure.

Another part of the witches' sabbath was sacrifice of some kind: at times, it was the witches sacrificing their bodies to Satan like a blasphemous nun ceremony, marrying him complete with intercourse. Later, this evolved into sacrificing babies, which would be abducted, ritually murdered, and boiled. Those present would drink the baby broth, which brought them ever closer to Satan's malevolent power. Such evil would empower the witches' own evil magic so they could harm others, cursing at will though again, this type of storytelling was an unconscious device to explain horrible luck in communities.

What we see is a hedonistic inverse of what Christians do and form of blood libel that was spread about witches anyway, especially during early modern witch hunts. A kind of casting off was done of the weirder parts of Catholicism and put on witches like the consumption of the blood and body of Christ. Witches were painted as the true monsters doing heinous things though the rituals aren't much different—even if the clothes stay on and wild folk dancing/orgy situations don't accompany the reverence.

## Modern vs. Movie Sabbats

The Wheel of the Year that includes Yule, Imbolc, Ostara, Beltane, Litha, Lughnasadh (also called Lammas), Mabon, and Samhain is used by modern witches and Pagans to celebrate shifts in the harvest year with cycles of birth, death, and renewal[ii]. Sabbats have been reclaimed more recently by modern witches reflected commonly in solo magical practice, though people do sometimes gather as a coven for these holidays. There is no naked copulation with Satan, demons, or orgies in the woods--merely celebrations for magical people rooted in past traditions of old and one's ancestors.

Movies tend to follow the sensationalized folklore of sabbats to a T. During these versions of the Witches' Sabbat, death, blood, and destruction meet on this momentous occasion for some form of transformation to take place. This is either in the form of cutting out the rot of corruption in a coven or women pledging themselves to Satan; there is also usually a calling of a specific girl to either lead them into a new unholy age or to join the coven because they were chosen. Most modern witch movies that feature sabbats are not interested in casting witches as the misunderstood characters they are; instead, they have devilry in their veins and they're ready to cause some mayhem. These depictions of the witches' sabbats are about destruction, renewal, and stepping into one's ungodly power. A bloody rebirth has begun because chaos reigns in these 3rd acts; the madness rises and falls once the task is done, and the ritual completed. These bloody ceremonies are a rebirth from a visceral womb; from the mania, a release from the mortal coil into a life enhanced by supernatural powers and what they believe is freedom. But are they truly free, or have they traded one patriarchal system of control for another?

# LORDS OF SALEM (2012) (Spoilers Abound!)

Heidi, a radio DJ, is sent a record that when played gives her flashbacks to Salem's past. She puts it on air and women all around the city go into trances because they are descendants of the daughters of Salem, just like Heidi. During the Sabbat after several strange experiences and trances, Heidi becomes who she's fated to be: the Satanic Virgin Mary giving birth to the Antichrist, surrounded by human sacrifices of the now-dead daughters of Salem. The witches had inserted themselves into her life and made sure she was primed for this role.

## Sabbat Scene

A theater is chosen to usher in the Antichrist, bathed in white light with the "whores of Salem" in dirty, 17th century clothing and symbols in dirt upon their heads. They bask in their nakedness, playing the unsettling Lords of Salem music on handmade instruments; these women were waiting for Heidi to complete the ritual. This moment paints the witches of Salem as emancipators who free themselves from mortality against the backdrop of neon-parking-lot-Christ imagery, likely intended to mock Christianity. During the ceremony, the women are moaning, yelling, touching Heidi's body as fluid flows from her vagina—it could be blood, could be urine, could be placenta, and it could even be all these things combined. The thing that she gives birth to looks like a cross between a spider and a lobster: it is writhing and clearly not human. The Sabbat ends with Heidi at the mouth of hell, hedonistic blood lust, and a sacrifice to Satan of 32 women's deaths, all who were descendants of the men that killed the witches in Salem. Heidi has disappeared.

### Bloodline Destiny

There is no real choice here for Heidi or the sacrificed women of Salem; they are slaves to the will of this evil coven and to Satan, powerless to stop anything once they hear the strange music on the airwaves. This is because they all have bloodline ties to old Salem, something they can neither run away from or change. The same goes for Heidi: it doesn't matter if Heidi wants to be the Satanic Virgin Mary—her bloodlines make it so and just like everyone else in Salem, she pays for her ancestor's mistakes that have nothing to do with her.

## SUSPIRIA (2018)

Susie is a shy ballet student, but during a Sabbat-like possession ritual, she discovers her full self: Mother Suspiriorum (Mother of Sighs), one of the lost mothers that's also a ruler of the witch world. The current leader of the witches, Mother Markos, has propped herself up as the lost third Mother to keep her power. Dr. Klemperer, a psychoanalyst, is drawn into the witches' web because the girl who went missing, Patricia, came to him for help before disappearing. Olga, another girl in the company, and Sara, are disturbed by Patricia's missing status, unable to accept the witches' explanations. Olga is murdered and Sara is trapped, forced into the ritual by magic. Dr.

Klemperer witnesses the ritual unwillingly as a victim.

Mother Markos desires a new body to possess—hers is diseased and disgusting, a physical manifestation of her corruption and abuses of power. Susie is chosen to be possessed but once Susie realizes that she is the true third mother and steps into her power, the jig is up. Death is summoned, kills Markos along with the other dissenters, and Mother Suspiriorum grants the girls who were unwillingly subjected to the rituals a soft, sweet death because they asked to die. The third Mother is orgasmic: blood is everywhere, and her transition to power is complete.

## Sabbat/Ritual Scene

The scene opens with weird, rhythmic breathing and women naked dancing in trance, some disembowelment, and increases in intensity like an orgasm; the setting is a barely lit room with hymnal-like song in the background. Susie follows the lights she sees down to the chamber, wearing a thin, see-through dress that shows her cleavage; the girls are dancing, possessed. Blanc waits in all red, with loud exhales all around, and everyone is naked—Dr. Klemperer is there too, also naked and cowering on the floor, proclaiming his innocence. Sara and a few others are disemboweled silently, unaware of it; Patricia's rapidly decaying body is also there, and Susie is ready.

The ritual is a singing one, with loud exhaling and done in a violent, bloody dance. Young and old are all part of the ritual together, some willing, some not. Blanc fears for Susie while Markos taunts the girl: "there will be nothing left of you inside—only space for me," but Susie talks only to Blanc, reiterating her willing choice. Blanc tells her that if she has a shred of doubt, she'll make her forget all of it, that she feels something is wrong, but Markos insists they continue. Markos suddenly murders Blanc because she's opposed Markos for too long.

Markos tells Susie to think of her birth mother, tells her to reject her memory of that "false mother" and expel her; "death to any other mother". After Death shows up, Markos quickly realizes Susie is not who she seems, and Susie reveals that she is the real Mother Suspiriorum, saying, "I am she".

Death kisses Markos and her insides explode; everyone who supported her is also kissed by death, dying the same horrible way. Susie continues to sigh, seemingly in pleasure; she opens her vaginal-looking chest space to bleed with the others, her flesh writhing in the open wound, and asks the possessed girls what they would ask of her. Both Patricia and Sara ask to die, so they are kissed on the side of their foreheads, and they die softly. Susie has the other girls continue the dance because it's beautiful to her; she dances with them in a completely blood-covered chamber.

## Stepping Into One's Power

Susie has no references or formal training but has been compelled to audition; she impresses the witches running the school with her raw talent. Susie is overcome with excitement and happiness that she'll eat, sleep, and breathe dance on top of studying under Madame Blanc. Under Blanc's tutelage, Susie begins to develop a mother-daughter bond and as she connects deeper to the source material, the girl even begins going off-book. Blanc prepares Susie for the possession through her dance training. It is this trust between them that finally allows Susie to blossom into her true self and to step into her full power as a witch, as Mother Suspiriorum. She summons Death to cut out the rot of Mother Markos that has grown in her absence. Her power is at its fullest during the ritual possession ceremony, but Susie-as-Suspirorum shows the women compassion who were forced to take part, letting them die because they asked to.

The strobe lights begin in red light; there is screaming, blood is everywhere, and bits of body matter. This purging of the coven of its rot is an orgasm for Mother Suspiriorum (Mother of Sighs), who literally opens her chest for her blood to join the others' blood on the floor. It seems to give Susie a choice and empowers her to accept herself as the third Mother, but also, her path was predetermined—she was compelled to go to this school, to step

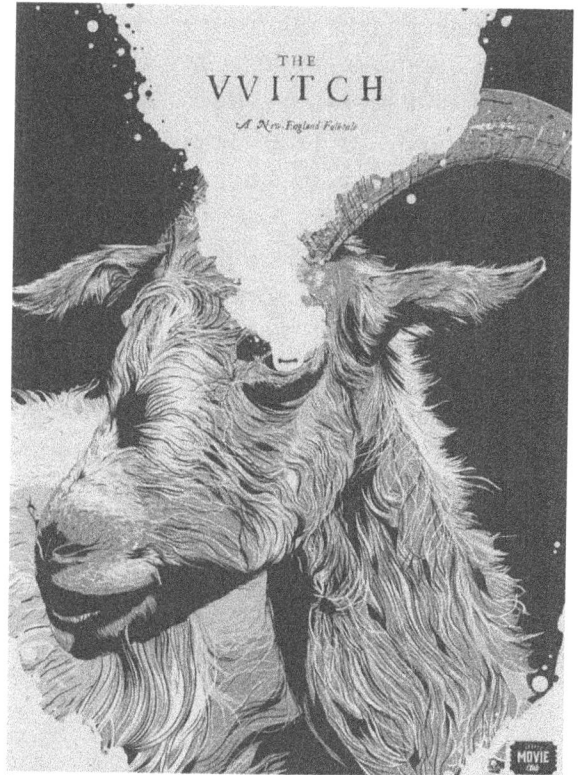

into her power fully as a woman. She seems happier as her full self.

## THE VVITCH (2015)

This movie weaves a tale of a family, banished and beginning anew along a forest they believe to be evil. Thomasin, the teenager, is leaned on heavily for the back-breaking work while things go wrong left and right: the baby, Samuel, is stolen when she had her eyes closed for an instant. Her brother disappears only to be returned on Death's doorstep, Thomasin's mother is consistently angry with her, and her twin siblings turn against her, which leads her father to suspect her of witchery. This culminated paranoia, forcing Thomasin to fight her family for her life and eventually, death befalls her entire family. In the young woman's despair, she turns to Black Phillip, a goat that's said to be the Devil; he shifts into a man, promises her she will live deliciously, and guides the girl's hand on the page to sign her name in his black book, tying her to him. She walks to the forest where a real Sabbat complete with nakedness, a written pledge to the Devil, and bloody nakedness. Thomasin rises into the sky, laughing semi-hysterically, with the other witches in the coven.

## Sabbat Scene

After all the levers were put in place to break her, Thomasin has no other option but to go to Black Phillip, bartering her soul with a single candle. Her family's blood is still splattered on her and Thomasin's hair is now loose and wild; she signs his book, removes her clothing at his request while the once-goat-now-man guides her hand to write her name because she can't write. Likely, the young woman cannot read either, so she doesn't know what she's signing up for. She then walks naked into the woods with only night sounds of the forest to accompany her; the girl comes upon angry-sounding chanting of the Sabbat around the fire—they are all covered in blood and the baby fat of her murdered brother, Samuel. Thomasin then joins them in their skyward

levitation, seemingly pleased with her new abilities.

## Slavery to the Devil

In this family of discontent and sin, it is only Thomasin that is the true innocent: she alone repents her actions to the Lord. What a boon it would be to the Devil to sacrifice the innocent lamb to evil. Thomasin was the true mark because sin lived too deep in the others: the father is Pride, the mother is Greed, Caleb is Lust, and the twins exemplify idleness and disrespect of their elders, breaking at least one commandment. With the right mechanisms, any soul could be pushed towards evil, the movie seems to say.

Riddle me this, Black Phillip: horned goat, Satan Himself: who doesn't want to live deliciously? All this horror to break poor Thomasin so she would sell her soul willingly to Satan. And yet, it was her family's sins that wrought this horror on her head. In this "New England folk tale", witches sacrifice a baby for its fat to rise in the air on broomsticks, sicken children, and pay a blasphemous price for their power. Puritans believed that all merriment was a sign of the Devil and that the pathway to Heaven was back-breaking work and to live in a kind of hell as repayment for humankind's sins. To reach the pure lamb in Thomasin, her entire family was bathed in their own blood as a sacrifice to the unholy earth. This was done to her; a nearby coven put mechanisms in place to break her family and steal her away until joining was her only choice. Witchery here is used as a metaphor for freedom from oppression but also the means of corruption in a pure soul.

When Thomasin gave in after all the horror, she traded in her servitude to God for a more literal form of slavery to Satan. This young woman signed her soul over to an entity she knows nothing about. What if he didn't deliver what he promised? Thomasin will be forced to do sick, twisted things to appease a horrible master that put levers in place to kill everyone she ever loved, to make her believe God had forsaken her. This land eats this family, spits them out, and steals their son; a place like this is not meant to be conquered.

However, Thomasin goes from serving one patriarchal master to another; though she is willing, she is not free. Thomasin is like a plumped pig for slaughter—we don't know what she'll be required to do for the Devil, nor does she since she likely cannot read the agreement she just signed. This is predator behavior, and the girl is his prey, but such is society to women. This, to me, isn't a "good for her" moment like many claimed of the movie when it debuted, but a young woman signing herself into a different kind of oppressive slavery establishment dressed up as her enjoying herself. She may have a good time during her exploits with pretty dresses, traveling the world, and the taste of butter, but Thomasin is also bound to the will of another for God knows how long.

## Conclusion

Though the act of embracing one's witch self is meant to be freeing themselves from the oppression of the mortal patriarchy, it looks like oppression in supernatural clothing to me. The wildness of the Sabbat is a shedding: the mortal coil, previous bonds, one's own humanity, and accepting into oneself the unholy power of the Devil along with indulging in the spoils of hedonism. That's why the blood and womb-like imagery is so prevalent: they are being reborn as servants of Satan or if he's not present in the narrative, accepting their full and true selves as magical. Much of the time, witches all seem to be working towards the goal of Hell on Earth and yet, it doesn't seem worth it—Satan's followers tend not to be rewarded well in these narratives because usually, they die or the Devil doesn't follow through with his promises. Satan is, after all, another man and once bound to him, the contract will be carried out one way or another.

# References

Dziak, Mark. 2023. "Witches' Sabbath," https://www.ebsco.com/research-starters/social-sciences-and-humanities/witches-sabbath.

Ellis, Bill. 2004. *Lucifer Ascending: The Occult in Folklore and Popular Culture.*

Ellis, Bill. 2000. *Raising the Devil: Satanism, New Religions, and Media.*

Friends of the Forest, "The Wheel of the Year". https://friendsoftheforestct.org/wheeloftheyear.

*Lords of Salem*, dir. Rob Zombie. 2012.

*Suspiria*, dir. Luca Guadagnino. 2018.

Tolbert, Jeffrey A., and Michael Dylan Foster. 2015. *The Folkloresque: Reframing Folklore in a Popular Culture World.*

Wikipedia, "Witches' Sabbats." https://en.wikipedia.org/wiki/Witches%27_Sabbath.

*The Witch*, dir. Robert Eggers. 2015

# TO HALT THE HEXENMEISTER

*Madness, Murder & Blood On the Bridge*

## SARAH BLAKE

The picturesque hamlet of Kenoza Lake, New York has charmed residents and visitors for centuries. Originally a location for boarding houses in the 1800s before transforming during the Catskill tourism boom, the region boasts stunning mountain landscapes, the community's namesake 224-acre Lake Kenoza, and the twenty-acre Stone Arch Bridge Historical Park. The centerpiece of the park is the triple-arched Stone Arch Bridge. Built by Swedish immigrants in 1880, the bridge has found a secondary home in countless pictures but what the photographers might not know is that infused into the bridge's seemingly peaceful stone is a complicated tale soaked in suspicion, madness, tragedy, and blood.

On the evening of January 19, 1892, local farmer Geroge Markert finished dinner with his family and decided to top off his evening with some friends at a "respectable roadside inn" called the Halfway House approximately a half mile from home. He arrived between 6pm and 7pm and enjoyed his drinks and company before leaving at approximately 11pm. When Markert's wife Katherine Zehner woke the next morning, she found that he had never come home, and she sent the pair's young grandson Johnny Markert to the Halfway House to ask the owner if he knew the whereabouts of his grandfather. Along the way to the tavern the boy ran into some neighbors, fellow farmer John N. Kohler and mail carrier Casper VonBerger and the trio walked together,

quickly arriving at the Stone Arch Bridge unaware their lives were about to change.

Blood. Lots of blood. On the stones, on the ground, and mixing with the footprints and large streaks in the freshly fallen snow indicating a struggle. The shocking scene suddenly became personal with the discovery of an open knife and a blood-soaked cap, but it was the chair leg that confirmed their fears. The chair leg was adapted to a walking stick years earlier and given to George Markert by the same grandson who recognized it immediately and was now staring at the crime scene. It was obvious that Markert was the victim of something horrible, but he was nowhere to be found. Kohler instructed young Johnny to go home and when he returned, he informed Kathrine "Pa is murdered and thrown over the bridge."

A search party of eighty people formed to try to find George Markert in the water under the Stone Arch Bridge. Boats made their way up and down the creek, moving the ice while others made their way up and down the riverbanks with rakes and hooks all hoping to find any sign of the man that no one believed deserved such a cruel end. For two days the party searched with no results until finally on January 22nd a constable in a boat saw something resembling fabric sticking out of the water. When they approached the fabric and used the hook the awful truth was revealed, the body of George Markert was pulled out of three feet of icy water and taken to the Halfway House to be examined by the coroner. Markert's body was brutalized before it was ever thrown over the edge of the bridge and into the icy water. There were eight lacerations on Markert's scalp from a blunt object, an eight-inch skull fracture, a large, bruised welt across his knuckles, and five bullets in his body all in the head, neck, and shoulder blades.

The murder of George Markert was terrible, but the aggression of the crime made it even more shocking. Markert lived less than 200 yards from the bridge and was well-regarded in his community. Born in Germany and moving to the United States in the 1860s he became a farmer and tended to the fifteen-acre farm where he lived with his second wife and children while being considered "honest and respected by nearly all his neighbors." He was also described as "an inoffensive man. Like the rest of the Germans, who make up the population of that vicinity, he enjoyed a glass of beer and minded his own business."

He was well-liked, but everyone knew there was one vital, dark truth simmering under the surface of this crime. It was something well known in the community. Markert had one enemy and when Johnny Markert, John N. Kohler, and Casper VonBerger arrived at the bridge Kohler immediately said what everyone already knew, "Well, if Markert is dead, Heidt killed him."

GEORGE MARKERT,

*Illustration of George Markert from the Middletown Times-Press.*

Adam Heidt was a forty-two-year-old local farmer and one that was very well acquainted with George Markert. The two men were former brothers-in-law from Markert's first wife, Adam Heidt's sister Caroline, who died shortly after the two were married. For many years Heidt spoke bitterly about Markert wishing him dead but the malice toward Markert was not tied to their farms. Heidt needed Markert to die because he was convinced that he was a "hexenmeister," or sorcerer who practiced black magic and that he was the one who hexed him and his family over two decades earlier.

According to Heidt it was in 1870 when he and Markert were both enjoying an evening at the Halfway House and Markert patted him on the shoulders while saying "You are a good brother-in-law, a good brother-in-law, a right good brother-in-law." The expression of this kindly remark is exactly when Heidt believed a hex was cast upon him and he claimed he was never the same after that night. The biggest problem was the illnesses. Headaches, facial pains, stomach issues, and crushing body aches seemed to plague Heidt and he visited doctor after doctor looking for relief but no matter what was done and no matter what medication was prescribed to him, he claimed nothing could cure him (some only made his ailments worse.) Doctors repeatedly told him there was nothing they could do, they could find nothing wrong with him. For ten years he found no relief, and at the same time he noticed other parts of his life that began to go wrong. Cows suddenly had blood in their milk, and the constant pain grew incessant. To Heidt there was only one explanation, and it clearly lay in malicious sorcery.

This belief that he had been cursed was heightened due to some specific instances in the presence of Markert. Until 1890 the two met at Heidt's house two to three times a year and during these visits he claimed that when he shook Markert's hand his pain flared up to a level that no medicine could relieve. He further stated that during one of these visits the two were drinking cider in his basement when

he began to feel a strange sensation in his face. When he looked in a mirror his face had taken on a yellow color and his eyes were lined in blue. After their beverages they went upstairs and that is where he claimed that Markert "stroked his whiskers and twisted his hand at the end of each stroke as if he was throwing something from them at me. He saw that I noticed it and stopped. When I turned my head, he did the same thing again."

With each visit from Markert Heidt said his pains increased, his face again became yellow with blue around his eyes, and his flare ups began to last longer, for days at a time. He told his wife that he believed to his core that everything he was experiencing was because of a hex from Markert. She did not believe her husband, pointing out that Markert was a religious old man but that did not matter to Heidt. What did matter to him was that nothing was going right in his life, doctors could not cure him, and that it all began with those words at the Halfway House "You are a good brother-in-law, a good brother-in-law, a right good brother-in-law." Additionally, there was a point in time where Markert lived in Connecticut for several years before moving back to New York and it was only during these few years that Heidt felt any relief from his pain only having it return to its full insufferable strength once Markert returned. Despite being in a constant state of pain he also believed that the curse of George Markert extended beyond him and into his family. Two years after the night at the Halfway House and the dreaded pat on the shoulders that he was certain ushered in his doom, Heidt's brother Nicholas died after he was hit by a train. Nicholas worked on the railroad and had been working on railway cars when Heidt believed that Markert possessed him to step in front of a train and be hit. In July of 1882 Heidt's father-in-law fell off a wagon and instantly died. In 1887 his mother-in-law was murdered by a former sailor named Abel John Allen. In Heidt's mind Allen was the murderer, but only because he too was possessed by Markert to commit the crime.

The last time Markert paid a visit to the Heidt home was December of 1890 and when the ailments persisted Heidt began to seek out cures outside the doctor's recommendations. Perhaps believing it was time to fight fire with fire, he began to consult witches and clairvoyants in New York City who all told him exactly what he already believed: You have been bewitched and what you need is not medicine, its revenge.

The advice and remedies given to Heidt from the witches and clairvoyants in the early part of 1891 became a silver platter to serve up the madness that would follow. After one hospital visit one told him he should not shake hands with any man and then gave him a piece of paper that he had to always carry with him but could never read. He saw this same witch six weeks later and received more unhinged advice that he believed, and hoped, would cure him. Parts of the advice were somewhat mundane, advising Heidt that he needed to boil a hat that belonged to Markert. He attempted to do this by having his twenty-two-year-old son Joseph approach the young Johnny Markert one day outside a market and offer him a quarter to take one of his grandfather's hats from his home and deliver it to him in the woods. Johnny went home and informed Mrs. Markert of the odd request, and she immediately said no. This was ultimately for the best, after boiling Markert's hat the second part of this remedy involved Heidt personally removing the brain from a dead man and boiling that as well.

All the delusions of Adam Heidt did not stay quietly within his own mind and George Markert understood his former brother-in-law believed him to be responsible for cursing him. Heidt wrote multiple letters to Markert threatening to take action but also threatening to take his life. One letter written in March 1891 references the earlier visit where Heid believed Markert was cursing him by stroking his beard at his house stating:

*"You seeming friend and sly enemy. Nothing done so fine but what it will appear in the daytime. God had opened my eyes. You should take your witchcraft back. You know I have a judgment against you. You came to me on a Sunday and got*

Article on the arrest of Adam and Joseph Heidt from The Sun.

a receipt. If you do not take the torture back, I will sell the judgment and pay the doctor bill which you have caused. You came to my house and stroked your beard. I was sick all the time. I forbid you my house and my barn, my flesh and blood. In the name of God. A Heidt."

At one point the content of the letters became so severe that Markert visited a judge and was told to prosecute, but Markert did not want to. He had no animosity toward Heidt and given their previous connection through marriage he felt best to leave the situation be. Another letter written to Markert from Heidt stated that if he saw him on his property he would be killed and in yet another Heidt said that if Markert did not stop "moonshining" his family he would kill him. These two letters were found in the pocket of the coat Markert was wearing the night he was brutally murdered on the bridge.

Everyone put the pieces together of Heidt being Markert's murderer, everyone except Heidt himself. When police arrived at his home he claimed that he had no idea about the murder, but the search of his house told a different tale. Found inside the home was a bloody handkerchief in a closet, an overcoat with blood spots, a 3.2 caliber pistol, and a bloody .38 caliber revolver with bullets matching the ones inside the skull of George Markert. Also found was evidence that he was not the only Heidt involved. His son Joseph had two large scratches on his hand, bloodstains on his clothing, and owned a pair of bloody boots with soles that matched the prints left behind on the bridge. The pair were arrested under charges of murder.

The trials of Adam and Joseph Heidt for the murder of George Markert took place separately with Joseph's taking place first on August 16th 1892. The jury of twelve heard the testimonies of George's widow Katherine, the young Johnny Markert, John N. Kohler who was with Johnny when they found the crime scene, the owner of the Halfway House Philip Hembdt, constables, his brother John, and others who made it a point to state that Joseph had an excellent reputation in town and never ran afoul of anyone.

Joseph sat listening to the accounts, dressed in black and sporadically bursting into tears. None of the accounts were going to save Joseph, he had already confessed to the crime in May 1892 when a judge visited him in prison.

When Joseph took the stand to tell his version of events the following day on August 17th his voice was barely audible. He spoke to the long-standing ill health of his father Adam and that he also believed his suffering was caused by a hex placed on him by George Markert. He fully acknowledged that he killed Markert, but he claimed it was done in self-defense. Joseph told the courtroom how he set out to confront Markert on that January night, not to kill him, but to beg him to remove the hex from his father. Joseph was George's nephew from his first marriage and when he found him on the stone bridge after being at the Halfway House he said he addressed him saying "Uncle, won't you please take that spell from father?" to which Markert responded with "I didn't put any spell on him and cannot take it off." According to Joseph he again asked Markert to remove the spell and was again told he did not place a spell so he could not remove anything. Joseph admitted he got angry and told his uncle he was going to have him arrested and he claimed this infuriated Markert who took out his knife. Saying he feared for his life Joseph then claimed he tried to

Article on the arrest of Adam Heidt from The Sun.

escape, but he slipped on some ice and when he grabbed his gun he accidentally shot Markert as he fell. He said he had no memory of firing five times, no memory of beating the man, and no memory of any further action other than throwing his body over the side of the bridge and into the water below. His account was murky, but he wanted one thing to be clear, despite everyone initially believing that Adam Heidt was the killer, Joseph was adamant that he acted entirely on his own and that his ailing father, who he truly believed was hexed, played no role in what happened on the stone bridge.

The jury deliberations against Joseph Heidt took just over three hours and at 7:40pm Joseph faced his fate. The jury obviously believed his confession of killing George Markert, but they did not believe he did so in self-defense. The verdict given

JOSEPH HEIDT.
JOINTLY INDICTED WITH ADAM.

ADAM HEIDT.
NOW ON TRIAL AT MONTICELLO.

*Illustrations of Joseph and Adam Heidt from the Middletown Times-Press*

was murder in the second degree with sentencing to take place two days later. But, Joseph would be back in court again before his sentencing, this time to testify at the trial of his father, Adam Heidt.

In many ways the trial of Adam Heidt was a repetition of the trial for his son. Beginning on the morning of August 18, 1892, much of the testimony was the same as what had already been stated and Adam sat in the courtroom listening while appearing very pale and ill. Witnesses spoke of the letters found in George Markert's coat pocket written by Adam Heidt threatening his life and multiple others told about Heidt's longstanding belief that his incurable mystery illnesses and multiple family tragedies were all caused by a hex placed on him by

Markert at the Halfway House so many years before. When Joseph took the stand he spoke about how long and how severely his father suffered from a vicious hex and described the countless ways he had tried to ease his suffering to no avail. He was still suffering, at the initial inquest shortly after Markert was killed Adam was asked if his ills were any less now that the man he blamed them on was dead and he stated "Not a bit. There is pain in me now. I saw Markert dead and saw Dr. Kemp extract the bullets from his head. The sight of him dead gave me no relief."

When all the witnesses were finished Adam Heidt's lawyer addressed the jury. He spoke plainly; this crime was one that his son Joseph was already found guilty of and stated that his father was not connected in any way. He asked that his client be acquitted on the grounds that there was not enough evidence to definitively tie Adam Heidt to the murder of George Markert in any way beyond speculation. The court agreed. When court reconvened the next morning of August 19th the judge advised the jury to find Adam Heidt not guilty on the grounds that there was not enough evidence that he was involved or that he even coerced his son to commit the crime. Without even leaving their seats the jury submitted a verdict of not guilty.

When Kohler stood on the bloody Stone Arch Bridge he stated "Well, if Markert is dead, Heidt killed him" and he was correct, but it was not the Heidt that everyone expected.

On the next day, August 19, Joseph Heidt was sentenced to a life sentence of hard labor and on August 22nd he began his time inside the walls of Dannemora Prison (formally Clinton Prison.) However, the life and times of Joseph Heidt did not end behind the prison walls, after twenty years he was released on parole for being a model prisoner and he was officially pardoned in 1914. Joseph went on to work for Malone Bronze Powder Works, married in 1925, and had a daughter. By all outward appearance he was able to rebuild his life, but some may say the darkness of 1892 never left Joseph Heidt. He took his own life in 1939, his body found hanging in his garage with a noose made from a clothesline.

After both he and his son escaped the death sentence Adam spent some time in Pennsylvania before returning home to Kenoza Lake months later. According to one report after his acquittal, he suddenly stated he was feeling better and told people he thought the spell might finally be broken. He may have felt better, but public opinion of him was far from optimistic with newspapers reporting that

## ADAM HEIDT ACQUITTED.

### JUDGE FURSMAN DIRECTS THE JURY TO GIVE A VERDICT OF NOT GUILTY.

#### Joseph Heidt's Strange Testimony of Markert's Black Art and Witchcraft.

Court convened in the Court House in Monticello at 10 o'clock Thursday morning for the trial of Adam Heidt for the killing of his brother-in-law, George Markert, in January last, his son Joseph having been found guilty of murder in the second degree for the same crime.

he was obviously dangerous to believe that "that poor old George Markert possessed the power of witchcraft, and by stroking his beard three times, and then spitting upon the ground three times could put a spell upon him that would impair his health and cause the death of his cattle. One capable of entertaining such a delusion is not a safe man to be at large. Now that Markert is out of the way, Heidt may select another victim unless put under restraint."

There was not much time for these opinions to simmer, in May 1893 Adam Heidt was again arrested and when he was told going to the State Hospital in Middletown would cure him he agreed to go. He never left the hospital. He was examined and found to be insane, officially committed to the facility on June 1st of that year. For four long years Adam Heidt remained at the State Hospital, eventually dying on July 22, 1897 from chronic melancholia and inflammation of the spine. He was only forty-eight years old

when he died and he had not had any contact with anyone in his family since he walked through the hospital doors. He also died before seeing that his family was far from done with tragedies. Of Adam Heidt's three sons two committed suicide and like Adam, one was also committed to an insane asylum. Both of his daughters died before the age of sixty and his wife Barbara died four years after him in 1901 after suffering from an illness.

When the murder of George Markert was discovered on the morning of January 20, 1892 the shock and speculation rippled through the community wondering why the farmer was so brutally killed and so unceremoniously thrown over the bridge into the water below. But what added to the tragedy was the motive when two men, fueled by paranoia, believed their family misfortunes did not come from the cruel hands of fate, but from the hands of George Markert when they laid upon Adam's shoulders three times and delivered a hex disguised in happiness.

"You are a good brother-in-law, a good brother-in-law, a right good brother-in-law."

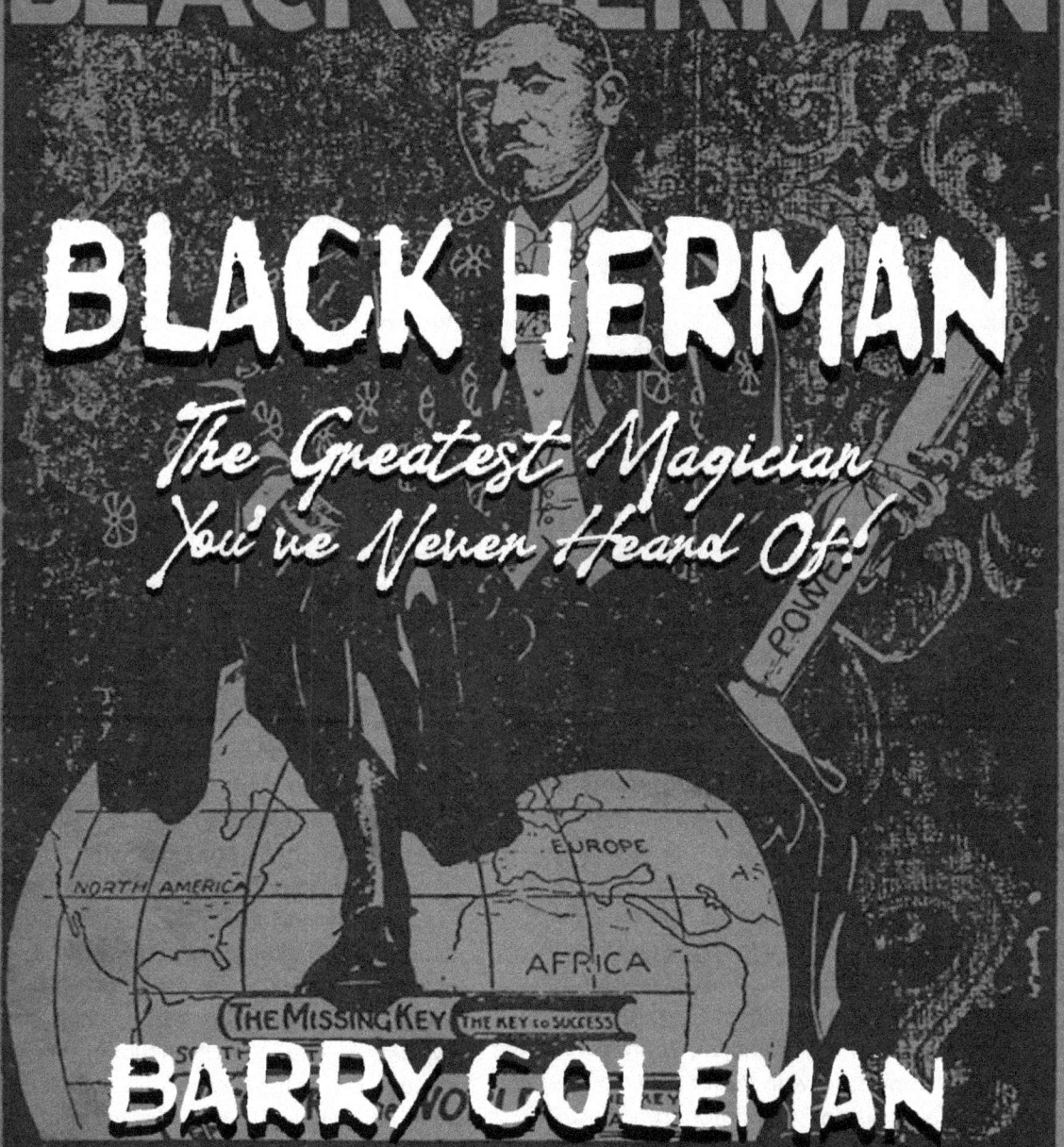

THE WORLD'S GREATEST MAGICIAN

BLACK HERMAN

BLACK HERMAN

The Greatest Magician
You've Never Heard Of!

BARRY COLEMAN

SECRETS OF
MAGIC-MYSTERY & LEGERDERMAIN
The Missing Key to Success, Health and Happiness

THE WORLD'S GREATEST MAGICIAN
BLACK HERMAN

SECRETS OF
MAGIC-MYSTERY & LEGERDERMAIN
The Missing Key to Success, Health and Happiness

Did you know that the first magician born in the United States was an African American? No? Well, neither did I, but his name was Richard Potter, and he was born in Hopkinton, Massachusetts, in 1783.

One version of his life states that he signed on as a cabin boy on a ship that ended up in the British port of Liverpool, where he attended a local fair. Fascinated with the sights, he was taken with a Scottish magician, John Rannie. He was so impressed with Potter that he hired him as his assistant. He later returned to America while in Rannier's employ.

Another version of Potter's story claimed that he learned the magical arts from a Signor Manfred while he was in Italy. He then returned to America with Manfred's troupe.

It's likely that the Rannie story is the closest one to the truth since records do exist that he did perform in New Orleans with Rannie.

In 1808, Potter was on tour in Roxbury, Massachusetts, when he met Sally Harris, a member of the Penobscot tribe. They were married and began to perform together.

In addition to being the first American-born magician, he may have also be the first homegrown "ghost buster," too. While at the Woburn Hotel in Massachusetts in 1827, he heard rumors that the room he was staying in was haunted. After examining the room, he discovered that a strange whistling noise often reported in the room was nothing more than the wind playing off a loose splinter in a beam in the ceiling. There were also sobbing and moaning noises, the stories said, but they turned out to be nothing more than doves, who also bumped and thumped against a rope in the ceiling as they struggled to get out.

Potter died in 1835 but during his life, he was so popular and respected as a performer that a town was named in his honor.

Although Richard Potter was the first African American magician, the most famous was undoubtedly the man who performed under the name "Black Herman." Born Benjamin Rucker on June 6, 1889, in Amherst, Virginia, little is known about his origins, especially since Rucker told audiences a variety of exotic – and fictional – back stories. In his own self-published 1925 book, *Secrets of Magic, Mystery, and Legerdemain by The World's Greatest Magician, Black Herman*, he claimed to have been born into the Zulu tribe and spent his childhood in the jungles of Africa. An old woman in his village predicted that he would become the marvel of his age.

He said that he'd been brought to America by a missionary when he was 10 and unable to adjust to civilized life, he ran away to Amherst, Virginia, where he worked for five years before roaming the mountains and forests of the region. He learned to communicate with animals and mimic wildlife, especially the birds. He claimed this helped him to become skilled at impersonations and ventriloquism – all part of his journey to becoming a humble and omnipotent god. (humble?)

Perhaps the humble part came during the next stage of his life, when he opened a small but successful lunchroom, then became a contractor in Lynchburg, Virginia, before entering business school in Cincinnati. Ever restless, though, he started traveling the world.

Taking many routes, he said that ended up in Egypt, a "country of mystery, that I was said contained all the secrets of the ages." Next, he ended up in India, where he made friends with great Hindu magicians. From them, he learned to place a person in a death-like slumber and bury them underground for eight days. Witnessed by a crowd, he unearthed the person and woke them up, finding them unaware that any time had passed or they had spent it underground.

After many weeks, he traveled to China, where he met up with a band of robbers. Knowing of his mystic powers, they tried to convince him to help steal a valuable jewel from a large statue. He refused, though, wanting nothing to do with the plot. Knowing he had raised the ire of the thieves, who feared he might reveal the plot to the authorities, he knew he was marked for death. He secretly selected a small vial from his collection of potions and after drinking it, became what appeared to be a lifeless corpse. News spread of his death and doctors were consulted, but there nothing to be done. Friends eventually reached the decision to send his body back to Africa, the king of the Zulu, for burial. Once his body arrived in Africa, a crowd of mourners surrounded his coffin and lifted the lid so they could look upon his body. Suddenly, his eyes opened, and he rose to greet the king. Everyone fled in terror, except for his younger brother and his mother, who put her arms around him as tears ran down her cheeks. Once again, his amazing powers had been proven.

While in Africa, he frequently helped his people. After a lion leapt from a thicket and carried away a young child, Herman chased after it into the jungle. When he caught up to the lion, he threw acid in its face and while the beast was distracted and pawing at its eyes, he pierced the lion's heart with a dagger.

He later saved the people when the village was surrounded by an enemy tribe. Using his great powers, he appeared to them as a red-eyed, fire-breathing monster, causing the enemy to flee back into the jungle.

Herman found himself in a precarious position when he was later seized by a tribe of cannibals, who placed him in a wooden cage where he would be fed and fattened up. Finding no physical way to escape, he turned to magic. To the dismay of the cannibals, he seemed to only become thinner each day until he was nothing but skin and bones. In disgust, the cannibals released him.

After that, Herman returned to American and worked as a detective in San Francisco. By turning himself invisible, he managed to solve the disappearance of a cook that had been abducted. He had learned this power, he explained, from Hindu magicians in India. It had been passed down from ancient Egypt.

When he began performing on the East Coast and Midwest, he drew huge crowds with his amazing performances. In towns without large buildings, he held revues in massive tents. Thousands of spectators, white and black, were thrilled by the carnival atmosphere, live music, Hindu magicians, and "gypsy" fortunetellers. But the star attraction was Black Herman himself.

He showed off his abilities to turn water into milk, to turn handkerchiefs into a large flag. And to produce ducks, rabbits, and chickens from mid-air. Volunteers tied him to a chair, using every kind of knot imaginable, but he was still unbound within seconds. He placed a female assistant in the "death cabinet," ran it through with several swords and caused "blood" to drip onto the floor, but, of course, the assistant stepped out, healthy and alive.

And what magic act would be complete without sawing a woman in half? His most spectacular stunt was suspending a woman in the air. He first put her into a trance and then as she became stiff as a board, he ran a sword around the platform to show there were no wires – and then caused her to disappear into thin air.

Black Herman was, in his own words, the "world's greatest magician."

But what was printed in that book was an "origin story," so to speak, that was a mixture of fiction and very little fact. It did, however, entrance his audience and they eagerly read his book, which also included simple illusions for novice stage magicians, advice on astrology and lucky numbers, and a sampling of African American Hoodoo folk magic and customs.

The real story of Benjamin Rucker wasn't nearly as exotic, but it is the story of a man who achieved great things at a time when the nation was bitterly divided over the subject of race. He grew up at a time when jobs for African Americans were limited, so he did what he could, like working on a farm and as a railroad cook.

He eventually made the acquaintance of a street magician named Alonzo Moore, who performed under the name "Prince Herman," and sold a snake oil patent medicine. Rucker became his assistant and was such a quick study, he was soon outselling his mentor. When he later went out on his own, he started calling himself "Black Herman" in honor of the man who gave him his start.

Rucker continued to sell a tonic, mixing the concoction from simple, readily available ingredients into what he called "Herman's Wonderful Body Tonic.". He would set up a cauldron and cook the mixture over a fire and suggest his customers toss a dime into the pot for good luck.

He drew in crowds by being tall, healthy, and well-built, and all his appearances were made wearing a tuxedo and tails. He knew that his image was crucial to his success. For a time, he promoted himself as Professor Black

Herman, claiming to have a Bachelor of Divinity and even going so far as to pay local ministers to appear alongside him. He also promoted himself as a faith healer and fortuneteller, grounding himself in Christianity while throwing in a little occult and Hoodoo for good measure.

As he gained a measure of fame, people began to question his act. Were those just tricks? Or was he in league with evil? He was accused of being a child of the Devil, or at the very least, having sold his soul for his magical skills. One Baptist woman said, "A man who can make a woman float in mid-air is no Devil, or pupil of the Devil. He must be Elijah the Second."

Black Herman, they said, must be either a devil or a saint.

It's no surprise that so many felt this way. At that time, African American religion was often tinged with magic, conjuring, Hoodoo, and a range of supernatural traditions. Hoodoo and Voodoo, often used interchangeably, are very different. Voodoo is a religious faith, linked to the Caribbean, while Hoodoo is a practice that delves into the lives of people and involves ghosts, spirits, and angels. It originated in Africa but has many variations, depending on the practitioner. The most sought-after practitioners were those born in West Africa and followed the Yoruba belief known as *ashe*. This is a belief that feels all things in nature, plants, animals, even inanimate objects have a spirit or soul. There was a hierarchy, with plants sometimes being the most powerful, with powers to harm or heal. These beliefs were integrated into familiar religious faiths to placate slave owners of the nineteenth century.

Hoodoo practitioners believed in an invisible world – it was a reality, not a theological abstraction. They believed that a force could morph into hexes, magic spells, and the creation of charms, amulets, and "mojo" bags, which were small bags filled with secret items that were blessed by a root doctor to ward off evil.

They mixed charms and potions, including what was known as "goofer dust," a lethal mixture that was added to dust scraped from cemetery markers. One of

*Benjamin Rucker, who gained fame as "Black Herman."*

the most coveted ingredients for any mixture was the bulbous High John the Conqueror root, which was used for many different things.

By the end of the nineteenth century, the former slaves and their children found themselves unable to get stable work in the South so thousands of them moved north to support themselves and their families. They settled in the larger cities, like St. Louis, Detroit, and Chicago, but being so far from home, many were left without the means to acquire the charms, plants, and powders they needed. There were pharmacies that could supply some of what was needed, but soon Hoodoo doctors began bottling a variety of their own mixtures.

Black Herman was one of them. He used Hoodoo to continue promoting himself, often claiming to be a descendant of Moses, a highly regarded religious figure who freed the slaves and was also considered the most powerful magician in the Bible. He'd not turned a staff into a servant, but he'd also magically parted the Red Sea.

He had been selling his tonics since the start of his career and now maintained a mail order business on the side that offered magic elixirs, three-color powders, lucky Mystic Oracle powders, and candles for love and fortune.

He also took his Hoodoo show on the road with him when he performed. For several years, he traveled through the South, providing healing remedies, reading cards, and divining fortunes. By the 1910s, though, he began running into problems traveling as a black man and he moved to Chicago.

It was in Chicago that Rucker met a performer named Wilmot A. Barclay, who had been born in Kingston, Jamaica. A skilled

*William Barclay, who performed under the name "Professor Maharajah"*

magician, he'd had trouble getting booked into many venues because he was black, so he put on a turban and passed himself off as a mysterious mystic from India, performing under the name Professor Maharajah. He was one of many African American performers who were forced to do this since they were often unable to get vaudeville bookings as anything other than as comic relief.

Barclay's career was allegedly a storied one. He supposedly coined the term "escape artist" and claimed he taught Harry Houdini how to escape from handcuffs when they performed together at a dime museum in Boston in 1895. He was also said to have escaped from a metal milk can before Houdini unveiled his version of the same trick a few years later.

In November 1906, Barclay made news after burying his wife underground for 104 hours. She was unearthed and found to be alive and healthy. It was Barclay who taught Black Herman the method of putting a person into a trance and slowing their heart rate and pulse so they could be buried for days in a catatonic state.

In the 1920s, he performed with another African American, Randolph Marcella, and his wife. They created a mind-reading act and topped it off with 15 illusions and escapes. The troupe toured together until Barclay passed away, although the date of his death is unknown.

After drawing huge crowds in Chicago and Detroit, Black Herman became set on performing in New York, even though friends and admirers tried to discourage the idea, believing his act wouldn't find receptive audiences there. But he was set on it and after gathering steam, took New York City by storm. Crowds flocked to see him, and he

(Above) Marcus Garvey

(Left) Liberty Hall

unexpectedly received a commitment to play at Liberty Hall in Harlem for 60 nights. He packed the theater and ushers sometimes turned away hundreds of people on various nights. Herman not only amazed his audience with magic, but he also handed out paper slips on which they could write questions for him to answer. He told people when or if they should change jobs, who had taken stolen items, and even united separated couples.

Liberty Hall was owned by the famous Marcus Garvey, a black national leader and racial activist who was born in Jamaica and came to the United States in 1916. He envisioned a Pan-African superpower and worked to form a publishing empire and the largest black political organization in American history. He offered lengthy speeches that enthralled African Americans with visions of freedom and success, while also soliciting his followers to invest in what he called his Black Star Ship Line, booking passage to return to Africa, their original home. Garvey's activism had been spurred by a trip he'd taken to Central America as a young man, where he witnessed the appalling conditions under which black men were working on the Panama Canal. He became a follower of Booker T. Washington, merging his philosophy with his own, which included metaphysics, spirit science, and occult beliefs from his boyhood in the Caribbean. Garvey and Herman would have made a powerful force if they had worked together, but regrettably, Garvey was later arrested for fraud.

But while performing in Harlem, Herman welcome guests onstage with him, including religious leaders, musicians, singers, and well-known speakers, who focused on the issues of the day, especially those facing African Americans. This was an era known as the Harlem Renaissance and so he mixed all these things into his act.

As his fame grew in New York, news of Black Herman spread from coast-to-coast. He began a national tour, arriving in cities and towns like a prince, bringing a large entourage and a reported $50,000 worth of equipment. Overflow crowds met him everywhere and while Herman made a fortune, he also gave back. He made quiet donations almost everywhere he went, funding scholarships, helping churches, and paying for school supplies in low-income areas.

He later purchased a brownstone at 119 West 136th Street in Harlem. The home, which had all the most modern conveniences of the

*A rare photo of Black Herman on the left side, holding the staff.*

day, was furnished with fine rugs, lavish furniture, and rare antiques. He also acquired a fleet of luxury automobiles.

But once again, he quietly gave to those in need. His door was always open to those experiencing hard times. He loaned money, helped with rent, paid for utilities, and made sure even the poorest families had groceries. He also established a Chautauqua Club, where men of prominence met with ordinary folks to discuss their experiences and offer words of wisdom.

Herman also held onto his occult roots. He continued to make tonics and elixirs for his mail order Hoodoo business, with his "Black Herman's Lucky Mystic Oracle Incense Powder" becoming his best seller. It was at this time that he also wrote his book that revealed both magic tricks and ancient secrets. All these things contributed to his growing fame and fortune.

He also continued to perform across the country and he and his brother, Andrew, created a mind-reading act that thrilled the crowds. There was nothing "psychic" about the act, though. Herman would send his assistant, Washington Reeves, to local cemeteries before his shows so that he could gather names and dates from the tombstones.

One evening, Herman and Andrew went to a graveyard to meet Reeves and found themselves surrounded by a group of thugs. When they recognized the famous magician, the men insisted that he pay them if he wanted to pass. Herman refused. He said that he only produced money using magic, as he did many other things – like raising the dead, for instance. Knowing his assistant was nearby, Herman raised his voice loudly: "Washington Reeves arise!" he called out in the direction of some nearby gravestones. Amid rustling leaves, a figure slowly rose from behind one of the stones.

Screaming in terror, the thugs fled from the cemetery.

As Herman continued to receive acclaim for his mind-reading act, he decided to expand on it by adding a female mind-reader to the show, a mentalist who called himself Madame Deborah. The two of them later ended up having an affair. Deborah was talented, though. She amazed the crowds with visions and predictions.

Herman was on tour in Mississippi when he noticed a pretty young woman named Eva in the audience. He was smitten and pursued her, too, eventually also adding her to the act as his assistant. Eva had a talent for tricks and illusions, and she became a permanent part of the show. Working with Professor Maharaja, she learned to perform the act where she was buried and then later exhumed.

On many occasions, Herman ran afoul of the law. White police departments were suspicious of a black man who made the kind of money he did in the 1920s and admittedly, many of his "private readings" and spells were questionable in their authenticity. It was during a session as a root doctor and spiritual advisor that a "lonely wife" visited him several times for help with winning back her cheating husband. Herman prescribed a mojo bag to wear around her neck, containing High John the Conqueror Root, scrapings from her husband's

Although it's difficult to make out, this is a rtare image of Black Herman performing his "Private Graveyard" stunt

shoes, and other things. He also told her to frequently recite a passage from Psalms. After she paid for his services, it was revealed that the woman was an undercover police officer, who arrested him for fortune telling and practicing medicine without a license. He was sentenced to a short stay in jail but claimed he escaped so often from his cell that the authorities couldn't have held him if he didn't allow them to do so.

But Herman never really regained his stride after his arrest. The country was dealing with the Depression and Harlem was hit especially hard. Money started to dry up, but Herman performed when he could, often ending up in front of small black audiences in the South.

This was when he perfected his most famous act – "Black Herman's Private Graveyard." He had been burying his assistant Eva for a while now. She had stayed in the grave for hours and days at a time, thanks to help from Professor Maharajah. But now he proposed burying three people at a time and scheduled this to occur at the Pythian Castle in Springfield, Missouri. However, a last-minute cancelation occurred when officials there worried about the legalities of the act.

Herman then decided on a different version of the act – he would have himself buried alive. It was quite the production. Herman stood in a wooden box and balled up a rag and jammed it under his arm. He said this would temporarily stop his pulse. When he stretched out in the box, he appeared to be dead to the spectators in the crowd. The lid was closed, the box was placed in a hole, and dirt was shoveled on top of it.

Days passed and finally, Herman was exhumed in front of an even larger crowd than the one that had watched him being buried. When the box was opened, Herman stepped out of it, alive, awake, and as fresh as the day he was buried. He was met with thunderous applause and rave reviews. No one could figure out how he survived – but he never had to. It was, of course, a trick. Herman hadn't been in the box for long. He'd had a little help slipping in and out of it and only had to lay low until his "resurrection."

By 1934, Herman picked up the pace, performing more shows and traveling to more towns than ever before. Some would later suggest he had a premonition of his impending death and that he was working hard because he somehow knew he weas running out of time.

But it might have been this hectic schedule that hastened his death.

Black Herman died on April 15, 1934, in Louisville, Kentucky, presumably the result of a heart attack – but not everyone was sure of that. The most popular version of his death stated that it happened while he was onstage at the Old Palace Theatre in Louisville. He collapsed but the stunned audience assumed it was part of the act. They knew about his "resurrection" act and tried to stop ambulance attendants who removed him from the theater. The police were needed to hold back the crowds.

But the real story was not so dramatic. Herman wasn't onstage when he died. He collapsed after eating dinner with his troupe at a boarding house in Louisville on Monday evening, April 14. Feeling sick on Tuesday morning, he stayed in bed but knew his end was near. He dictated several letters, including one to Eva in New York, detailing what should be done with his magic act.

His last words were reportedly, "I'm going to leave you all. I'm going away."

He died that day from what doctors stated was an infection of the heart.

Rumors spread after his death. Many claimed he was poisoned. Some claimed the culprits were members of his troupe, or he was poisoned by a jealous mistress or even on orders from J. Edgar Hoover, who was trying to control black activists.

There were many others who refused to believe Herman was dead at all. They were convinced it was all a publicity stunt. After his body was taken to the J.B. Cooper Mortuary, crowds formed outside, demanding that Black Herman show himself. Eventually, the undertakers agreed to place his body on display. Herman's managers concocted the idea to charge a dime for anyone who wanted to see the body before the burial.

He was later shipped to his family, where a traditional funeral service was held for him at the AME Zion Church in Harlem. Even with all his money, he was buried in an unmarked grave in Woodlawn Cemetery in the Bronx. He was only 45 years old when he died.

In the years that followed, scores of imitators tried to reproduce his illusions and acts, especially the Private Graveyard show. But none of them could match the talent and skill of Black Herman. He was not only a great showman, but a great businessman at time when African Americans had fewer rights and faced even greater prejudices than today. In addition to his generosity, he provided work for more than 40 people, ran a mail order business, an herb farm, and printing shop. He also brought black labor groups together with governmental offices as part of the National Recovery Administration established by President Franklin D. Roosevelt. His fame and public image paved the way for black performers that followed, including Louis Armstrong, Ethyl Waters, and many others.

Con man and charlatan or African American activist, showman, and benefactor, Black Herman was truly a tireless man who is almost completely forgotten today.

NEW FROM TROY TAYLOR!

THE MAN FROM BEYOND

HOUDINI AMONG THE SPIRITS

TROY TAYLOR

# THE
# WITCHING HOUR IN
# SPRINGFIELD

## MICHELLE FISHER

*Illustration from The History of Springfield in Massachussetts (1921)*

The story of witchcraft in 17th-century New England is often framed through the dramatic lens of Salem in 1692, but earlier cases, such as those in Springfield, Massachusetts, during the 1650s, offer an equally revealing window into the social, legal, and emotional landscapes of early colonial communities. Unlike the later infamous trials, Springfield's witchcraft accusations emerged not through the presence of professional witchfinders, but from the complex interplay of interpersonal rivalries, moral anxieties, religious expectations, and the pressures of frontier life. Examining these events requires a nuanced understanding of the historical sources, the emotional and social context, and the mechanisms by which fear and suspicion crystallized into legal action.

The chain of events in Springfield began with incidents that might appear mundane, yet which were interpreted through the lens of spiritual warfare. Domestic misfortunes became amplified into supernatural signs: for instance, the Parsons household experienced repeated disruptions, such as food inexplicably spoiling or puddings bursting in the kitchen. These ordinary mishaps were interpreted as evidence of malevolent forces acting through human agents. In the tight-knit and morally vigilant environment of Springfield, even minor disruptions could quickly be transformed into indictments of witchcraft.

Mary Parsons, a central figure in the accusations, was described by witnesses as exhibiting unusual behaviors that raised alarm in the community. Reports surfaced that she had "marks of the devil" on her body—a term used in 17th-century New England to refer to unusual blemishes, moles, or other physical signs thought to indicate a pact with Satan. Hugh Parsons, her husband, became entangled in the accusations not only through association but also because of his perceived emotional detachment and moral failings in the eyes of the townspeople. Observers noted his failure to express sufficient grief when his son died, a detail which would later play a pivotal role in legal proceedings and in shaping his reputation.

Martha and Rebecca Moxon, children in neighboring households, experienced convulsions and fits that were attributed to spiritual assault. Such behaviors, now understood through modern medicine as potentially neurological or psychosomatic, were interpreted at the time as signs of demonic influence, often linked to a specific accused witch. These incidents highlight the interplay between the everyday and the extraordinary: Springfield residents lived in a world where the natural and supernatural were constantly intertwined, and misfortune was often moralized and personalized.

The Parsons case demonstrates how suspicion could emerge from the intersection of domestic incidents, social visibility, and the moral expectations of Puritan society. In Springfield, gossip, observation, and fear created a feedback loop: one incident amplified anxiety, which in turn heightened the scrutiny of individuals, leading to more accusations.

The legal framework for addressing witchcraft accusations in 17th-century New England was both sophisticated and frustratingly limited. Witchcraft was considered a "secret crime" overseen by the devil, which meant that direct evidence was rarely available. For a case to succeed in court, authorities required material proof, such as "devil's marks," or credible eyewitness testimony. Massachusetts law also required multiple witnesses, presenting a structural challenge: if witches operated in secret under the devil's supervision, how could reliable evidence be gathered?

In Springfield, Mary and Hugh Parsons were subjected to examinations for such marks. These procedures were informed by English precedents, including the 1648 case of Margaret Jones, a midwife executed in Boston after witnesses reported her in the company of familiars and bearing devil's marks. These early New England practices mirrored English trial procedures in seeking tangible evidence, even as they struggled with the inherent elusiveness of the crime.

The legal proceedings themselves involved extensive depositions and interrogations. William Pynchon, Springfield's magistrate, gathered testimony from multiple witnesses, meticulously recording their accounts. Witnesses described in detail the behaviors and appearances of Mary Parsons, her interactions with neighbors, and the alleged malefic acts attributed to her. One deposition recounts a neighbor witnessing her in the company of a "black creature," interpreted as a familiar spirit, while another describes her performing actions thought to manipulate supernatural forces over the household's fortune.

Hugh Parsons' role in the proceedings was complicated by his perceived stoicism. During his son's death, observers noted that he did not display the expected public grief. This was interpreted as emotional abnormality and as potential evidence of hidden guilt or complicity with the devil. The case illustrates how emotion—or the lack thereof—became a form of social and legal evidence.

Reconstructing life in Springfield requires careful attention to multiple types of sources. Birth and marriage records in order to track family structures, fertility, and child mortality, all of which reveal the social foundations of the community. Town maps illustrate property ownership and the spatial relationships between households, shedding light on unneighborly networks and points of tension. Account books and other administrative records illuminate economic relationships, debts, and obligations, particularly involving figures like William Pynchon, whose authority extended across both financial and social spheres.

Central to this reconstruction are depositions from witchcraft trials. These documents, often dense and difficult to read, provide direct insight into accusations, interrogations, and the responses of those accused. By reading from these we can discern not only the overt narrative of the trials but also the rhythms of daily life, patterns of consumption, and subtle cues about social norms and interpersonal dynamics. For example, a deposition from 1655 notes the frequency of visits between households, complaints about unpaid debts, and social conflicts that may have exacerbated suspicion, providing a granular picture of the underlying tensions that fueled accusations. These archival encounters reconstruct mentalities, social hierarchies, and emotional states that might otherwise remain inaccessible.

Witchcraft, by nature, occupies a liminal space between the real and the imagined. Understanding it requires imagining the mindset of individuals who believed themselves under spiritual assault, while avoiding the pitfalls of fictionalizing their experiences. As Stuart Clark notes, witchcraft is "a subject with a hole in the middle"—a real-world phenomenon infused with supernatural meaning that resists straightforward reconstruction.

One of the most striking aspects of the Springfield cases is the role of emotion in both accusation and defense. The history of emotions has emerged as a crucial tool for understanding early modern life, revealing the ways in which communities interpreted, judged, and regulated behavior. In Springfield,

emotional display was a form of social evidence. Hugh Parsons' perceived lack of grief at his son's death became a central accusation against him, highlighting how normative expectations about emotion could be weaponized.

Emotions also functioned as a medium of social communication. Anger, envy, guilt, and fear were projected onto others, turning personal feelings into public claims. Witches could be seen as repositories of collective anxieties, embodying social tensions in ways that were both symbolic and practical. Accusations thus reflected both individual behavior and the broader moral and psychological climate of the town.

For instance, the Parsons case demonstrates how envy and economic rivalry could intersect with accusations of witchcraft. Some witnesses accused Hugh of hoarding resources, manipulating debts, and exploiting neighbors, behaviors amplified in testimony as evidence of spiritual malfeasance. The overlap between moral, economic, and spiritual concerns made witchcraft accusations particularly potent social instruments.

Geography amplified these effects. Springfield's location on the edge of the wilderness contributed to a sense of vulnerability and existential threat. Settlers contended with isolation, wildlife, and the possibility of Native American attack, creating a heightened awareness of danger. Such conditions likely intensified the imaginative and emotional dimensions of witchcraft suspicion, making minor incidents appear potentially catastrophic. Witnesses often described hearing unexplained noises at night, or seeing strange movements in the surrounding woods, which were interpreted as signs of supernatural activity.

Religious belief also shaped the perception of witchcraft. While Springfield was not uniformly Puritan, the influence of Puritan teaching was significant. Ministers like William Pynchon preached godly doctrine, emphasizing vigilance against the devil's work. Puritanism itself was characterized by tension— an awareness of moral failure, a suspicion of hidden enemies, and a focus on spiritual discipline. These concerns made communities particularly sensitive to deviations in behavior or emotional expression, framing everyday life in terms of spiritual struggle.

Yet Puritanism in Springfield existed alongside pragmatic concerns, including economic competition and personal ambition. Residents were expected to maintain moral rigor while navigating a highly competitive social and material environment. Witchcraft accusations can thus be read as both moral and social instruments, regulating behavior and reinforcing communal hierarchies.

For instance, Pynchon's own records reveal tensions between moral expectation and economic reality: some townspeople resented the authority of those who held financial sway, interpreting conflicts as moral failings or evidence of witchcraft. Similarly, the Parsons' case illustrates the double bind of Puritan expectation: failure to publicly demonstrate proper grief or piety could be construed as evidence of hidden sin.

The repercussions of witchcraft accusations extended beyond the accused. Children of those prosecuted were often socially "stained," even if legally exonerated. Reputation, household stability, and social capital were intimately connected to the outcomes of trials. In some cases, the stigma could persist across generations, shaping family trajectories and social standing long after the immediate legal events had passed.

In Springfield, records suggest that children of the Parsons family faced social marginalization. Neighbors avoided their households, marriages were delayed or obstructed, and economic opportunities were constrained. While not prosecuted directly, these children inherited a social burden tied to accusations against their parents. This underscores how witchcraft accusations functioned as instruments of social control, regulating behavior not just for the accused, but for entire households and kin networks.

A useful point of comparison is the work of Matthew Hopkins and John Stearne in East Anglia during the 1640s. Hopkins and Stearne acted as catalysts, identifying pre-existing suspicions and encouraging the collection of material evidence. In Springfield, by contrast, accusations arose organically from within the community, rather than being driven by external professional witchfinders. This difference emphasizes the role of local social dynamics: Springfield's cases were generated by interpersonal rivalries, moral anxieties, and frontier pressures rather than by the presence of itinerant witch-hunters.

Nonetheless, the underlying mechanisms were similar. Both contexts exploited pre-existing fears, tensions, and mistrust, showing how witchcraft accusations functioned as a form of social regulation. In East Anglia, the intensity and brevity of the witch-finding campaign highlight the fragility of these processes: even with professional intermediaries, suspicion could only be temporarily mobilized before social and legal pressures restored equilibrium. Springfield's accusations, though less dramatic, illustrate the same dynamics on a smaller, more intimate scale.

# BEWITCHED IN CLOUD CITY

## ERIN TAYLOR

*The Leadville gallows- 8-10,000 gather for a double hanging (not the vigilantes) in Leadville 1881.*

Tabor became the mayor of the new town of Leadville and aimed to bring culture to the lively town. He relocated his house off Harrison Avenue to make space for what he envisioned as the greatest opera house on this side of the Mississippi River—the Tabor Opera House. Built along Harrison Avenue in just 100 days, the opera house was equipped with gas lighting; a testament to Tabor's wealth. However, ticket sales were disappointing on opening night November 20, 1879, as many townsfolk preferred to witness the vigilantes' double hangings down the street at the jail. Despite a disappointing opening night, the opera house eventually hosted notable figures such as Oscar Wilde and John Philip Sousa. There are even rumors that the great Harry Houdini performed there, as the trap door was sized to his specifications. However, there is no actual evidence that he ever visited Leadville.

By 1879, Leadville had a population of 20,000 residents. State Street (now Second Street) was known to be an area of town where no one wanted to walk alone, especially at night. This was a scene of the rough-and-tumble Wild West, known for brothels, saloons, theaters, and violence.

Pneumonia was a leading cause of death, ahead of mining fatalities, suicide/murder, health complications, overdoses, and other maladies. The City Cemetery was established at the end of Chestnut Street, just outside of town, with the first burial occurring on November 17, 1877. By May of the following year, an estimated 250 graves were already placed within the one-acre site, and action needed to be taken.

Nestled in the picturesque Rocky Mountains of Colorado, a quiet mountain town has the serene nickname of "Cloud City," sitting at an elevation of 10,154' above sea level... the highest incorporated city in the United States. The town was settled after the discovery of silver in the mines and made some millionaires overnight. Many flocked to the mountain town in hopes of striking it rich, and many left despaired. Some didn't leave at all, becoming residents of the local cemeteries. Ghost stories were whispered among folks from early on, and then there were those who spoke of another supernatural entity... witches.

Before Leadville was established in 1878, Horace Tabor was a general store owner who lived in Oro City with his wife and son, hoping to strike it rich. One day, he overheard two miners in his store discussing their claims and offered his assistance in exchange for a share of any profits—a practice known as grubstaking. His gamble paid off when silver was discovered, making Tabor wealthy.

Before the end of that year, Evergreen Cemetery was designated for burials on the north end of town. Many bodies from the City Cemetery were relocated, but the issue arose that the original caretaker was inadequate at record-keeping. When he passed away, all knowledge of grave locations was lost. In a manner reminiscent of the film *Poltergeist*, grave markers were moved, but the bodies remained in place. Today, a historic marker stands at the site of the City Cemetery, and it is unknown how many of Leadville's former residents lie beneath.

*The current view of the city cemetery.*

In 1886, when Si Minich was hanged at the gallows outside the cemetery, his execution was witnessed by an estimated three to seven thousand spectators. Before he was buried in the pauper's section of Evergreen Cemetery, local newspapers reported that his ghost was already haunting the local jail.

For years, his grave in the pauper's section was marked only by a simple marker that read "Hung." However, it was soon noted that the grave seemed to be losing dirt; either the ground was sinking or something—or someone—was digging above his coffin. Speculation arose in the 1898 *Herald Democrat* regarding a woman who practiced "hoodoo" or black magic. It was said that she made potions in her kitchen, and she allegedly scooped up dirt from the murderer's grave to scatter at the doors of those she wished to curse. After three nights of spreading the dirt, the curse would take effect. Some townsfolk gathered on the third evening to intervene, but the supposed witch disappeared into the darkness when confronted.

Who was this mystery woman?

One woman was brought before a judge for witchcraft in 1899. Locals claimed to have seen her at Si's grave, gathering dirt to channel negative energy at those who had wronged her. Some even alleged that her eyes rolled back and shot fire into the night sky. Stunningly beautiful Catherine Rothenberg was known for making accurate predictions and knowing fortunes—for a small price. When Martin Roberts tried to challenge her, asking for mining advice, he was amazed by her response. He rushed home to share the news with his wife, but she was not as impressed. Mrs. Roberts stormed over to the Rothenbergs, accusing Catherine of fraud. In response, Catherine threatened the physical and mental health of the Roberts family, leaving everyone to wonder what the outcome would be—if anything at all.

That night, Martin's head throbbed, and he believed he must have been under the spell of

Catherine Rothenberg from the
Colorado Transcript

the beautiful witch. He later told a courtroom that she once informed him that the only way to counter a curse was to bleed her mouth. In a fit of desperation, he broke into her house to assault her. "My power is gone!" Martin Roberts was charged $30 for the act of "blood-letting," and Catherine moved to Denver, with no further reports of her practicing witchcraft.

There was speculation that Catherine may have been a clairvoyant or medium, as many were drawn to Spiritualism at the time. Spiritualists frequently traveled through Leadville, boasting of their abilities to communicate with the dead. Newspaper critics of the time often labeled someone a fraud, pointing out gimmicks or illusions; however, certain spiritualists managed to impress the crowd, especially when they revealed information they should not have known.

Many walks of life came and went in search of their dreams, some worked hard, and some may have cheated...and some may have dabbled in a little witchery. In 1893, the Silver Panic shook the town when the value of silver significantly dropped. Many people, including Horace Tabor, experienced the shift from rags to riches and back again. As a result, many left Leadville searching for new wealth, while some stayed for various reasons. The cemeteries became populated with lovers, dreamers, criminals, and paupers, with supernatural residents lingering and waiting. Keep an eye on the shadows, you just don't know who is waiting to gather dirt.

Leadville, 1900

# VANISHED IN BROAD DAYLIGHT

## THE HAUNTING CASE OF T.J. DAVISON

## ADAM WHITE

# He was just four years old. No one saw a thing.
# And no one ever asked why.

October 10th, 1985, began like any other fall day in Decatur, Illinois. The leaves were changing, the wind was crisp, and life in the quiet Midwestern town carried on with its usual rhythm. Nestled three hours south of Chicago and a little over two hours north of St. Louis, Decatur was a place where neighbors greeted each other by name and families gathered around dinner tables every night. But by early afternoon, everything changed. By 1 p.m., the heart of Decatur was filled with fear. A four-year-old boy had vanished, and nothing would ever be the same again.

That afternoon, Delany Davison drove to the Kroger in Brettwood Village with four children in tow: her own child, two of her nephews, and four-year-old Timothy Jacob Davison—known simply as TJ. He was a sweet, quiet boy with a gentle spirit and a shy smile, and on that day, he had fallen asleep in the back of Delany's red Dodge Omni hatchback. It was 1985—a time when people didn't think twice about leaving a child in a car for a few minutes while running into the store. Delany made a decision that would haunt her for the rest of her life. She left TJ in the backseat while she took the other kids inside for groceries, leaving the car unlocked.

She returned just 25 minutes later. But in those short, fleeting moments, the world turned upside down. The car was still there. The doors still unlocked. But TJ was gone.

Panic set in immediately. Delany's mind raced—was he hiding? Did he wander off? But the more she searched, the more the realization set in like ice in her veins: TJ had disappeared. No one in the busy parking lot had seen a thing. No one had noticed a boy in a blue windbreaker and white sneakers being taken. No one had heard a cry or seen a struggle. It was as if TJ had been erased from the world in an instant.

Police arrived quickly. Officers combed the grocery store, nearby businesses, and surrounding streets. Helicopters flew overhead, scanning rooftops and woods. Delany and the children were questioned repeatedly. She told police that earlier that morning, she had dropped off the older kids at school, taken TJ and one other child back

# Boy missing

**By ELAINE SHELLY**
Herald & Review Staff Writer

Police were searching Thursday night for a 4-year-old boy last seen sleeping in his aunt's car in the Brettwood Village Kroger store parking lot.

Police believe that Timothy "T.J." Davison is missing, but they are not discounting the possibility he was abducted.

Timothy's aunt, Delaney Davison, who takes care of him, left him in her car because he was sleeping, and took three other children into the store to buy groceries. When she returned to the car 30 minutes later, about noon, the boy was missing.

The search halted late Thursday after police and the K-9 unit searched a wooded area near True Value Hardware, 2809 N. Main St. Police say they searched the entire north end of Decatur using police officers on foot, police dogs and a helicopter. Police say if Timothy is not found, today's search will most likely retrace the areas covered Thursday.

Timothy is white, with dark brown hair and eyes. Thursday morning, he was wearing a light blue windbreaker, a black baseball cap, blue jeans and tennis shoes. He is about 3-feet-4 and weighs 40 pounds. He answers to Timothy or T.J. and does not know his last name. His speech is not clear.

After police circulated pictures and information about Timothy on Thursday, they received several reports from Decatur residents saying they had seen a little boy wandering around in the Brettwood Village area and across U.S. 51. Police have been unable to determine if any of the callers actually saw Timothy Davison.

Police have contacted Timothy's mother, Debra Deloach of Winter Haven, Fla. and were trying to contact Timothy's father, Dreyden Davison, also of Winter Haven, to see if they know where the boy is. Debra Deloach said she did not know where Timothy is.

Twenty Decatur police officers searched for the boy in the Brettwood area on foot. Some police officers walked through the Brettwood parking lot showing pictures of the boy and asking shoppers if they had seen him.

Police stationed in the Brettwood Village area were not the only ones involved in the search. Decatur-Macon County I-SEARCH distributed a flyer carrying information and two pictures of Timothy. Information about Timothy was called in to the state I-SEARCH computer.

Sharon Rametta, manager of Super X, a drug store next to Kroger's, spent time looking for Timothy after the Kroger manager informed her of the missing boy.

"We searched the store (Super X) and then I got in my car," Rametta said. When she drove down U.S. 51 she spread the word about Timothy to some construction workers in the area.

Timothy "T.J." Davison in June 1985 photo

home, then brought them all to Kroger later around lunchtime. TJ had been asleep on the floorboard behind the front seat, too tired to move. None of the children had seen him leave the car. No one saw anyone suspicious. There were no signs of forced entry, no struggle, no clues.

The sense of dread only deepened. Officers knocked on every nearby door, searched the wooded area along Stevens Creek, and investigated the public aid office behind the village. They checked the swimming pool, the local Best Western, Miles Chevrolet, and even the construction zone at the new bridge project. TJ's photograph was distributed to every store. Still, nothing. Every lead turned cold. No one had seen a boy matching his description. It was as if he had simply vanished into thin air.

At the station, Delany cried uncontrollably, her hands shaking as she turned over custody documents and power of attorney forms. The guilt weighed on her like lead. Her voice cracked as she explained that she only left him for a moment. Just a moment. The children were interviewed separately. Her 7-year-old daughter hadn't even been at the store; she'd been at school all day. TJ's five-year-old brother told police that yes, TJ had stayed behind in the car, still asleep, when they went inside. When they came back, he was gone. The youngest, just two years old, was too young to understand, too young to help.

As the first night fell, the town of Decatur held its breath. TJ was somewhere out there—he had to be—but where? And with whom? Search teams expanded their reach. Police officers worked around the clock. The community came together in fear, confusion, and hope. But with each passing hour, that hope grew fainter.

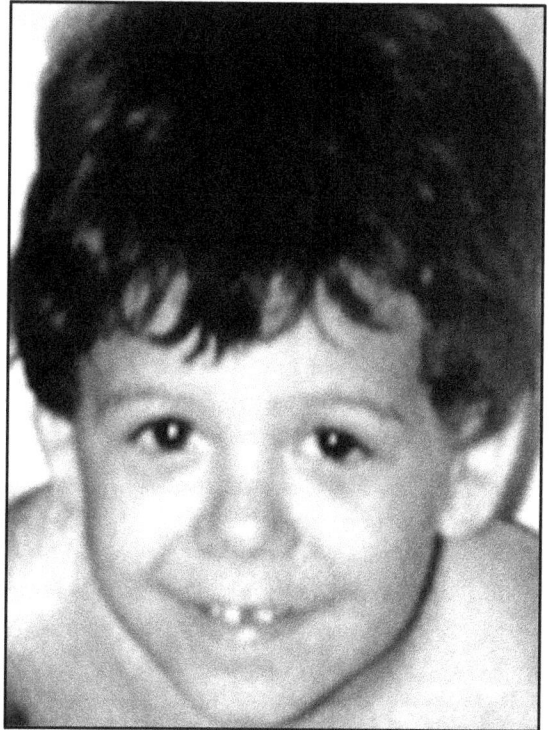

TJ had been born on a cold January morning in 1981 in Peoria, Illinois, to Debra and Dreyden Davison. His early years were marked by silence—he suffered from a speech delay that made it hard for him to communicate, which only deepened his gentle, quiet nature. His world was already complicated. His parents' relationship had fallen apart. In the years before his disappearance, the family fractured. TJ and his siblings were passed from household to household, first to their grandmother, then to Aunt Delany in Decatur. The children lived in her modest home on North Charles Street, where things seemed calm—but unsettling questions lingered.

Just one day after TJ went missing, police reached out to his father, Dreyden Davison. He never showed up for questioning. Then, on Sunday, October 13, he was arrested in Winter Haven, Florida, in a bar—picked up on

# Missing Decatur boy's case rekindled

**T.J. Davison disappeared 28 years ago at age 4**

By NICOLE HARBOUR and CHRIS LUSVARDI
H&R Staff Writers

DECATUR — Nearly 28 years after a Decatur boy disappeared, police said Friday they have been actively investigating the case again.

The Decatur Police Department, assisted by the FBI and Macon County Coroner Michael E. Day, began digging up an empty lot Tuesday at North Charles Street and Harrison Avenue.

Police detectives, along with the FBI Evidence Recovery Team, have been searching for evidence related to the 1985 missing person investigation of Timothy Jacob "T.J." Davison, said Lt. Jason Walker, head of the Decatur Police Criminal Investigations Division.

Davison was 4 years old when he disappeared in Decatur on Oct. 10, 1985.

The search concluded Friday, Walker said. Walker did not say what evidence might have been recovered, as the investigation remains open.

The reason for the search is based on a complete review of the past investigation, rather than a specific tip, Walker said.

T.J. Davison's aunt, Delaney Davison, who had custody of him, told police the boy was sleeping in her car when she went shopping in a Brettwood Village grocery store. Returning to her car 30 minutes later, she said T.J. had vanished.

Despite countless hours of police investigation, numerous news stories and several calls from people throughout the country who believed they had seen T.J. or someone who resembled him over the years, he has not been found, and no

**MISSING/A2**

Macon County Coroner Michael E. Day, with bucket, and law enforcement officers work at a digging scene Tuesday at North Charles Street and Harrison Avenue.

*Herald & Review/Hugh Sullivan*

Colorado Springs. Jersey City. A boy was spotted in Mexico who looked just like TJ. He was hearing-impaired and mute, communicating only through drawings of a plane crash—

unrelated assault and battery warrants. The Decatur police and Florida authorities questioned him about TJ, but his answers were vague. He claimed he hadn't seen his son. There were unconfirmed rumors he'd been in Decatur around the time of the disappearance, but nothing stuck. His alibis didn't quite hold, but no physical evidence tied him to the case.

Meanwhile, TJ's mother, Debra, still living in Florida, was also questioned. Her life, too, had unraveled since the divorce. She clung to hope that somehow, her son might come home. When a group of missing children was discovered in Tallahassee in 1987, one of the boys bore a striking resemblance to TJ. Debra stared at the photos for days, heart pounding, but it wasn't him. Another cruel twist in a story already full of heartbreak.

Rumors spread like wildfire. One tip claimed TJ had been taken by a cult for a ritual sacrifice. The informant had a long history of mental illness, but some details matched things police had already heard. Investigators followed up. They searched, dug, questioned—but again, it led nowhere.

Over the years, leads came from all over the country. Wilmington, North Carolina.

again and again, the same image. There was a moment of hope, of breathless belief. But it wasn't TJ. Just another ghost.

By the mid-1990s, TJ's name had nearly faded from the headlines. A few newspaper articles, a couple of interviews—but the case was growing cold. That would change in 2013, when nearly 28 years after TJ vanished, the FBI returned to Decatur to investigate the vacant lot where Delany's house had once stood. The house had burned down in 2002, and with the city now owning the land, police didn't need a warrant to search.

A cadaver dog swept the property and alerted—there were traces of human remains. Hope surged again. Special Agent James Krueger with the FBI's Evidence Response Team arrived and began probing the site. A void in the ground, previously noted by police, was marked for excavation. Officers stood guard around the clock.

On July 9, 2013, the digging began.

Rain delayed the work for several days. But eventually, the earth gave up its secrets. Bones were found—carefully bagged and sent to the coroner. Family members gathered near the site, watching in silence, whispering among themselves. Every piece of dirt, every bone fragment, was examined by anthropologists.

Possum bones. A cow bone fragment.

Nothing human. No TJ.

The search was over. Again.

And just when it seemed like the story couldn't grow any darker, fate struck another devastating blow. Two years after TJ disappeared, his aunt—Cindy Lee Smith—also vanished.

In April 1987, Cindy was last seen by her boyfriend, William Donald Taylor, in Winter Haven, Florida. She had a six-year-old son and plans to move back in with her parents. But she never made it. Her mother, Elsie, reported her missing days later, but police did little. Weeks passed before anyone even contacted the family. Then, rumors began. Taylor had been seen selling Cindy's belongings. Cindy's father stormed his house, and what he found sent chills down his spine: her mattress, stained with blood. It was turned over to police. But at the time, DNA testing wasn't advanced enough to offer answers. Years later, the mattress was thrown away. The one piece of evidence that might have held the truth—gone.

Taylor's stories shifted over the years. He claimed she left with a stranger. That she went to Daytona Beach. That she just walked away. But others swore they saw her getting into his car that night. In 2007, he died—taking the truth with him to the grave.

Cindy left behind everything: her car, her dogs, her tax refund check, and most hauntingly, her son. The boy would grow up motherless, with more questions than memories. Just like TJ.

Two disappearances. Two lives erased. Two tragedies too close for coincidence, and yet, authorities never found a connection. Still, the parallel haunts the family—and the town.

Today, 40 years later, TJ's case remains unsolved. The town that once clung to hope has grown quiet. Time has moved on, but the questions haven't. Was he taken by someone he knew? Did a stranger slip away with him in broad daylight? Or did something darker happen in that car, that home, that family?

What's strange—almost chilling—is that in all the decades since that October afternoon, there have been no new leads. No follow-ups. No reporters knocking on doors. No public requests for information. Not from his mother. Not from his father. Not even from the aunt who was with him that day. No renewed searches. No statements. No desperate pleas for justice.

Nothing.

And it's crushing.

Crushing that a little boy could vanish without a trace and almost no one in his family has ever demanded answers. Crushing that the people who should have shouted the loudest have gone silent. It makes you wonder—was TJ even in that car that day? Or did something else happen to him, something far more disturbing than anyone has ever admitted?

Is it possible that someone out there knows the truth... and has chosen to stay silent all these years?

TJ never got the chance to grow up. Never learned to ride a bike, to start school, to speak his truth. His voice was silenced before it ever had the chance to be heard. All that remains is a missing child's face on an old flyer, yellowed by time. His name is spoken less and less—but for those who remember, he is not forgotten.

The people of Decatur still ask the question. They always will.

What happened to TJ Davison?

And why has no one said a word?

The Spiritualist movement got its start in America in 1848, when the Fox Sisters began speaking to spirits in update New York. The movement took the country by storm and soon men and women across the nation were making money and achieving fame as they began helping ordinary people to speak to their dead loved ones – or were they?

From the very beginning of the Spiritualist movement, there were magicians and investigators who were adept at re-creating the allegedly "miraculous" phenomena of the mediums. They would do so by duplicating, then exposing, their effects. The methods practiced by the mediums were simple, these men claimed, and were merely stage illusions just like the ones being created before audiences in vaudeville theaters across the country. Many of these performers thrilled audiences with recreations of what believers were experiencing in the séance room. They included professional magicians like Harry Kellar, Howard Thurston, and, of course, Harry Houdini.

"If I can only get your attention intently," one magician claimed, "an elephant could pass behind me, and you would not see it."

By the late 1920s, the investigation of spirit mediums by magicians had started to decline. After the death of Houdini in 1926, only one man came forward to carry on the work that Houdini had been doing. Joseph Dunninger was a friend of the late illusionist and, in addition to his reputation as the "world's greatest mentalist," he also became one of the last true magician and paranormal investigators. Others came in his wake, but he was the last of the breed that approached the unexplained with an open mind --- and admitted that there were some things he wasn't able to explain.

Dunninger was born to poor German immigrants in New York's Lower East Side in April 1892. His life changed when he was seven years

*Joseph Dunninger*

old, and his father took him to see magician Harry Kellar at the Academy of Music. He became entranced with the mysterious and went to see both spirit mediums and numerous stage magicians. He was determined to become a conjurer himself and saved his money to buy apparatus and magic books.

At the age of 16, "J. Dunninger" began performing on the stage, presenting a sleight of hand act at the Lenax Club. Two years later, the "Mysterious Dunninger" was offering card tricks, "Oriental Mysteries," and illusions of spirit séances on the same bill with boxing matches at the Masonic Temple in Brooklyn. He was working hard to make his name known in the competitive field, but he also had to earn a living, so he took a job at John Wannamaker's department store, first as a messenger, then as a stock-room clerk, and then as a comparison shopper. During this time, he was also setting a record for the longest consecutive show for any magician to play in New York -- 65 weeks at the Edsen Musee, a wax museum on West Twenty-Third Street. The hall was torn down shortly after Dunninger closed in 1915.

After this, Dunninger accepted offers from a couple of traveling vaudeville shows and toured the country for the next several years. Dunninger's career continued to rise, and he became known for what other magicians called "his unusual and interesting method of handling the art of magic". Even his mentor, Harry Kellar, stated at a banquet for American magicians that Dunninger "would become one of the greatest conjurers the world has ever known."

The more that he performed, though, the more he began to realize how interested audiences were in his mind reading and mentalist stunts. Thanks to the press coverage that he received for several such stunts -- especially ones that he did to raise money for War Bonds -- Dunninger began to study methods for convincing his audience that he could secretly access their thoughts. To enhance his act, he became a student of Eastern studies and cultivated his interest in the occult and

*Dunninger with Houdini, demonstrating a spirit trumpet*

psychical studies. He didn't realize it at the time, but this became a turning point in his career, and he soon became known as one of the greatest mentalists of all time.

Dunninger studied the methods of many other "mind reading" acts of the past but all of them seemed to need one thing that Dunninger did not --- an assistant. He planned to offer his act alone and he perfected his new approach in 1919, playing the role of a researcher who had made an important discovery. Performing for the Press Club in Boston in 1920, he introduced himself as the president of the invented American Psychical Society.

Newton Newkirk, a *Boston Post* columnist, wrote an article after the demonstration, telling of the man who had stated, "mind reading was a science." On the night of the Press Club appearance, Dunninger distributed squares of paper, inviting his audience to write names, dates, or words on them, and then to fold them and put them in their pockets. He then instructed a volunteer to gather just five of the folded papers. According to Newkirk, the professor (as he referred to Dunninger) then produced an empty envelope and asked the volunteer to place the papers inside of it. The man tucked them inside, without Dunninger's help, and then Dunninger closed the envelope, tossed it onto the floor and asked the volunteer to put his foot on it and keep it there.

Dunninger then stepped back from the audience and sat down behind a table

that concealed him from the audience below his elbows. He explained that he could read human minds more readily if all the minds in the room were on the same level as his own. He then stunned the group by easily reading exactly what had been written on the five pieces of paper in the envelope.

Soon after stories of his Press Club performance appeared, more

ORPHEUM THEATRE
Easton          Matinee Saturday
FRI. & SAT. JAN. 22-23

DUNNINGER
The master mind of modern MYSTERY

accounts were printed of even more dramatic feats. Dunninger astonished the staff of the *Evening Record* by spelling out the words in a headline chosen by the editors. He found a key that was hidden by the staff of the Houghton & Dutton department store and singled out one person, in a crowd of 3,000 assembled in the Boston Common, whose description had been written down and stored by a committee. These fantastic happenings in Boston led to a command performance of mind readings at Steinert Hall, which, despite the August heat, was filled to capacity.

Billed as "The Man That Read the Mind of Mayor Hylan", he received top billing at a benefit show at the New York Hippodrome in 1921. In smaller type, the advertisement noted that the most famous athletes in the country, Babe Ruth and Jack Dempsey, would be his subjects. In the years that followed, Dunninger became famous as a society entertainer, performing for audiences and celebrities all over the country, including four United States presidents -- Calvin Coolidge, William Howard Taft, Warren Harding and Theodore Roosevelt. During a party in Long Island, he also performed for the Prince of Wales, discerning the name "Johnny" that the prince had written on a paper in his pocket.

As his popularity grew, he began to book shows that would earn him as much as $1,500 per performance. His mind reading act puzzled and mystified audiences and skeptics alike, although he always maintained that it was done simply by illusion and that no supernatural powers were at work.

Houdini's announcement that he was leaving vaudeville to tour with his own full evening of magic in 1925 was followed by a press release from Dunninger, saying that he, too, was going to front a theater mystery attraction. This was not uncommon at the time, even among friends, for it was a highly competitive time for magicians and magic shows often crossed one another as they toured the country.

Dunninger opened his show of "Bewildering and Astounding Effects and Spiritual Creations which have Never Been Offered to the American Public" at the Opera House in Philadelphia in June 1925, but as it turned out, the rest of the tour was postponed until the following year. He closed his big show in early 1926 and signed a contract to headline in Keith vaudeville houses with his mentalism act. He proved that he could baffle audiences in Boston, Baltimore, Washington and on Broadway in New York. After that, he went on to head Orpheum billings in the west.

By this time, sellers of magical secrets were offering explanations as to how Dunninger was performing his baffling act in Keith theaters. Dunninger took note of this in the November 1927 issue of *Science & Invention* magazine. Drawings at the top of one page showed a performer palming slips of paper as he helped spectators put them in envelopes, then later opening the slips of paper

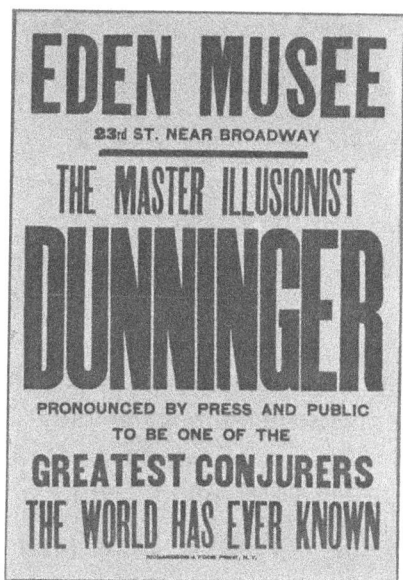

*Dunninger posters from around the country, as well as a Dunninger Magic Set for kids*

under the cover of a pad. Dunninger flatly denied this was his technique and undoubtedly, many readers believed him. Magicians admired him for his sheer audacity.

Around this same time, Dunninger became the chairman of the Committee for Psychical Research, which was established by *Science & Invention* Magazine. Dunninger had recently announced in the New York Times that he planned to carry on "Houdini's work of exposing fake mediums." The magazine decided to post a prize of $1,000, which would be paid to any medium who could produce phenomena devoid of trickery, or which could not be duplicated by natural means. The offer of only $1,000 did not last for long. It was soon increased by several $10,000 awards until the money for

genuine spiritualistic demonstrations finally added up to a total of $31,000.

Dunninger was picked to lead the committee of investigators, which would include scientists and several prominent magicians, and contestants had to abide by the following conditions:

1. The contestant had to be a practicing medium, making supernatural claims to the manifestations to be presented. They could not use conjurer's tricks or optical illusions. Therefore, the performances of magicians, or those not claiming Spiritualistic powers, could not be considered. Such tricks would not be accepted as evidence.

2. Contestants had to be willing to undergo tests or their manifestations at

the New York offices of *Science & Invention* at 230 Fifth Avenue.

3. The same committee of investigators that witnessed the tests of mediums would also witness the tests that the magazine would stage to duplicate the phenomena or manifestations in question.

4. Automatic writing would not be considered. Tests such as these were

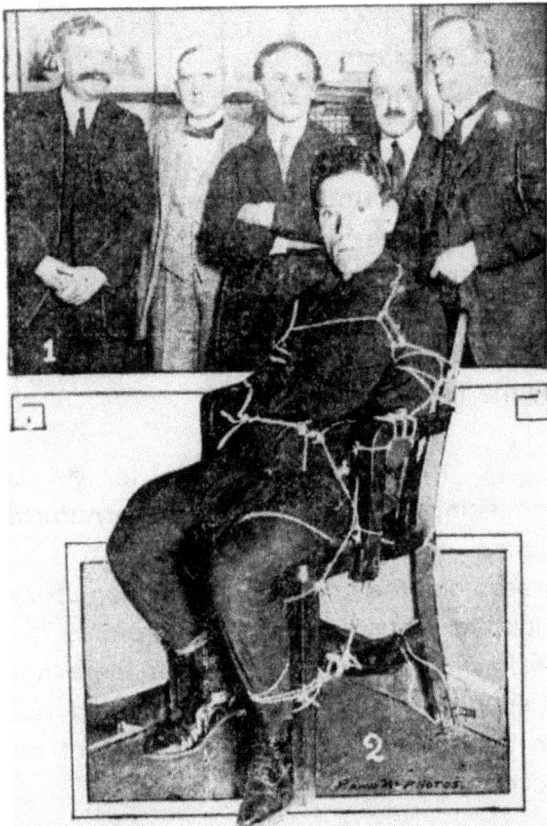

*One of the mediums that Dunninger exposed during the magazine contest was Nino Pecoraro*

considered to be subconscious phenomena.

5. Mediums had to consent to present their offerings before the staff of Science & Invention investigation experts, general press representatives and Joseph Dunninger.

6. No exposés would be published in the magazine as to the methods employed by the practicing mediums in the contest, as it was Science & Invention's desire to expose nothing other than fraud and self-deceptions.

7. Methods employed by telepathists, mind readers and mental artists would not be accepted as evidence of spirit force.

8. If preparation time was needed for duplicating a medium's effects, such as time for building or creating the necessary apparatus, the necessary time had to be granted by the contestant.

The conditions went on to say that if a tie occurred, both contestants would be awarded a matching prize and if no contestant emerged as a genuine medium, the prize money would be withdrawn. Editor Hugo Gernsback wanted to make it clear that it was not the intention of the magazine to ridicule those who believed in spirit manifestations. He only wanted to show that most such happenings could be duplicated by natural means and were not sufficient to prove that supernatural phenomena were the actions of the dead. "Up to this time," Gernsback wrote, "there had not been any scientific basis to prove conclusively by scientific means that there is a communication between the deceased and the living."

Hundreds of mediums applied but, in every instance, Dunninger was able to recreate any phenomena they offered. Soon, mediums throughout the country began to insist that the magician was a medium in his own right. They claimed that he had occult powers, but Dunninger insisted this was not true. "Any child of 12 could do what I do," he often exclaimed, "... with 30 years' experience!"

One of the most dramatic exposures to occur during the committee sittings was that of Italian medium Nino Pecoraro. Just one week after Pecoraro tried unsuccessfully for the award, Dunninger, tied up just as the medium had been, produced a glowing, ghostly form, lines written in Houdini's handwriting, and wax impressions of a spirit hand. Pecoraro's manager, who was present for the "séance", insisted that Dunninger himself was a medium, which the medium denied. A short time later, Pecoraro appeared at a press conference that was called by Dunninger and signed a confession admitting that the manifestations that he had performed for Sir Arthur Conan Doyle and others were fraudulent. At the press conference, he demonstrated how the manifestations had been created.

Even though he was able to duplicate the manifestations that had been presented to the committee, his writings showed that he had not given up hope in the genuineness of the spirit world in general:

"The hope which springs eternal is responsible for a great extent for the widespread credence given to Spiritualism, as well as for a number of other beliefs and practices. It is not at all the purpose of the present writer to decry Spiritualism in itself; for since man lives here below, there is always the possibility that he may exist in another world which he enters after death. Perhaps some day conclusive evidence will appear that will hearten all mankind, and explain the mystery of life and death which has bewildered us ever since the world began."

In July 1929, Dunninger ventured into radio with a series of "Ghost Hours" that originated at WJZ in New York. Although extensively publicized, the series did not attract much of an audience. He continued to earn high fees, though, with his shows and he kept his name in the papers by continuing to reveal the tricks of fraudulent mediums.

In March 1943, he made another try at radio at KYW, Philadelphia, with a new type of program. This one was a smash hit and that fall, he began a regular 6:30 p.m. Sunday night show on NBC's Blue Network. The show used the same techniques that

DUNNINGER, exponent of mental telepathy, is shown above in the act of transmitting thoughts by Radio. In a recent test through the NBC he projected one of three thoughts to 55 per cent of his audience.

Kem-Tone Miracle Wall Finish PRESENTS

## DUNNINGER

### GREATEST MENTAL MARVEL OF THE AGE!

ON THE Kem-Tone

## MIRACLE SHOW

### KGA 6 P. M.

TONIGHT—AND EVERY WEDNESDAY NIGHT

*Dunninger took the radio waves by storm, offering a modern version of his act, which he then recreated on television.*

had been so popular on stage and Dunninger became a sensation. Slips and envelopes were passed out before the program went on the air. Listeners heard him as the WJZ studio audience to concentrate. He called out the first letters of names. When someone said that he was thinking of those initials, Dunninger, letter by letter, spelled out the names. Audiences were thrilled.

The program was switched to a better time, 9:00 p.m. on Wednesday night, in competition with comedian Eddie Cantor and singer Frank Sinatra. *Life* magazine devoted eight pages to Dunninger, the new phenomenon on the air, on March 13, 1944. Not since Houdini had a magician so intrigued the American public.

Dunninger changed with the times. He progressed from radio to television in 1948 and became one of the few stars to ever have a series on all three major networks. His on-air feats continued to be described as "awe-inspiring and more than a little disquieting."

On television, as on the radio, Dunninger featured his "Brain Busters" act. He probed secret thoughts as remote cameras showed an officer on a submarine whose "mind was being read" or a man and woman "concentrating on secret answers" as they parachuted over Coney Island. When not appearing before the cameras, Dunninger was performing for live audiences or gathering material for magazine articles and books. There was no hint in his book *What's On Your Mind?*, which was ghost-written by Walter Gibson (who also prepared books for

Thurston and Houdini and created the pulp series "The Shadow"), that Dunninger was not a genuine mind reader. In fact, the book contained experiments for those who wanted to develop their ESP abilities and described how to hone mind reading skills in detail.

While praising Dunninger as a showman, magicians had been criticizing him for years for claiming to have true telepathic powers. Dunninger laughed and told reporters that if magicians knew how his act was done, it was strange that they were not duplicating it.

When one did, though, and began appearing on network interview shows in the middle 1960s, Dunninger was furious.

George Kresge, Jr., who became famously known as "Kreskin," became fascinated with the comic strip adventures of "Mandrake the Magician" when he was just five. By the time he turned 15, the lanky young man from New Jersey, who wore horn-rimmed glasses and had a friendly manner, was giving professional shows. He performed mental feats that were eerily similar to Dunninger's in town hall and on lecture circuits. Kreskin made frequent appearances with Mike Douglas, Joey

*Dunninger continued to perform very late in life, mostly because he wanted to make sure that audiences knew that the so-called "Amazing Kreskin" had stolen his act.*

*Dunninger with Lucille Ball*

Bishop and other television hosts. He moved into night clubs, theaters and concert halls and even marketed a bestselling game that used a pendulum to answer questions that were posed to it. He billed himself as "The Amazing Kreskin."

Dunninger, whose 1956 ABC series had

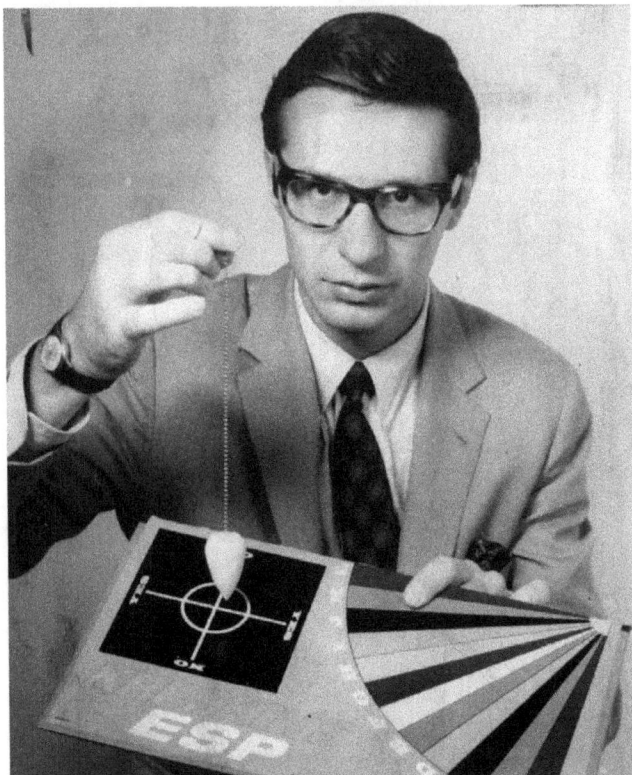

*The "Amazing Kreskin"*

been titled "The Amazing Dunninger," noted with increasing irritation that Kreskin was not only using his techniques, but often his exact words. In January 1972, "The Amazing World of Kreskin" began airing and Dunninger, now 79, became even more distressed. It's true that Kreskin's show was a watered-down version of what Dunninger had done, offering minor celebrities when Dunninger had worked with stars like Gary Cooper, Lucille Ball and Jack Benny, but it was still too close for comfort to the aging magician. Kreskin also sat in a chair doodling on a pad, just as Dunninger had done when he was "tuning in on a spectator's thoughts" and Kreskin, also, explained that he wore his glasses because he couldn't see the notes he made on the notepad without them.

Kreskin remained popular for years while Dunninger began taping his final television series at WPIX in New York in the fall of 1967. A few years later, illness forced him to retire.

Dunninger died in March 1975, after decades as an entertainer and investigator. He was the last of the great showman and investigators to pass on and he left a wonderful library of books and articles on magic and the illusions of the spirit mediums.

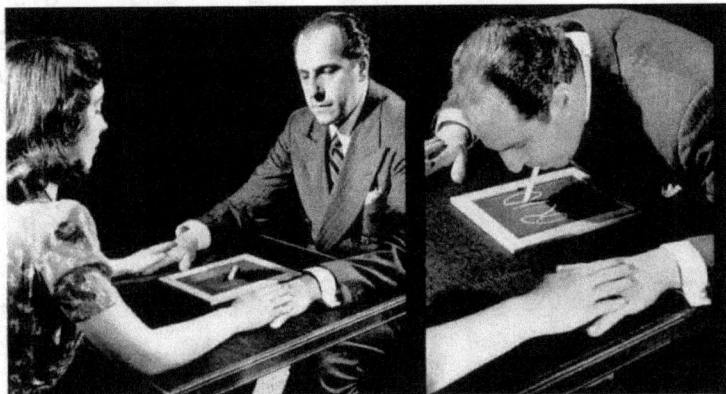

DUNNINGER
The master mind
of
modern
MYSTERY

# THE MORBID CURIOUS NO. 12
# CONTRIBUTORS

## Susan A. Jacobucci

"Sue," Susan A. Jacobucci, hails from Somerville, Massachusetts, USA. She is an independent researcher and founding associate of K & S Paranormal with her investigations taking her to haunted locations in the Midwest and Eastern United States. Sue's most recent articles, one about a haunted town hall published in Sam Baltrusis' *Haunted Travels Anthology*, Volume 1, June 2025, and another titled, "Haunted Sentinel 1.4.3 (I Love You!)," about a ghostly lighthouse published in the most recent edition of *Morbid Curious*, Number 11, Haunted Hometowns Issue. Sue has published other paranormal articles in Volumes IV, VI, and VII of *The Feminine Macabre* and archaeological pieces that have appeared in American Antiquity, Archaeology of the Northeast, and The Bulletin of the Massachusetts Archaeological Society. Sue earned a Masters in Historical Archaeology, a Bachelor of Science in Anthropology, and a Bachelor of Arts in Sociology.

## Victoria Jaye

Victoria Jaye is an author, podcaster, and writer in the paranormal / horror analysis genres. Her book, *The Black Hours: Modern Demonic Experiences & Folklore* expanded her master's thesis work from Utah State University. Victoria's podcast, Demon Folklorist, can be found on Spreaker and on several other podcasting platforms where she talks about demons, folklore, and horror movies. Her research interests are demonic narratives, experiences, phenomena, and media. Victoria also analyzes horror movies for her column, The Novelty Shoppe, on Morbidly Beautiful. She is currently expanding her research into classifying other types of negative supernatural experiences.

## Sarah Blake

Sarah Blake is the creator of HushedUpHistory.com and recently released her first book, *Hushed Up History Volume 1*. She has contributed more of her true tales of dark history to the book series *The Feminine Macabre* Volumes 1-7 and to

*The Morbid Curious* No. 10 American Blood Issue. A lifelong lover of all things strange and unusual, the last decade has included writing about the forgotten chapters of history, devouring and investigating the paranormal, painting nightmares, studying Tarot and mediumship, and working in a crematory and various museums. She drinks too much tea, buys too many books, stays up too late, and is owned by six cats.

## Barry Coleman

Barry still lives in the same 174-year-old house, with his wife, and part-time entities who have identified themselves as Robert, Frank, Betsy, Ann and someone with the last name Talmage. They all say hello. Coincidentally and unintentionally, they made an offer on the house on Friday the 13th and took possession (pun intended) on October 31.

## Michelle Fisher

Michelle Fisher is a teacher living in Oxfordshire in England. With a lifelong passion and interest in the paranormal Michelle created Haunted History Chronicles Podcast in October 2020 to combine and share some of her passions and connect with other like-minded individuals. Michelle has been featured in *American Paranormal Magazine*, *Unknowing*, *Haunted Magazine*, *A View Beyond*, the *Mortiferous Muse Zine*, *High Strange*, *Ghost Mag*, *Myth* and *Lore Zine*, *Morbid Curious* as well as in Volume III and VI of *The Feminine Macabre*.

## Erin Taylor

Erin Taylor is the proud parent (errgh) author of six books, with the recent publication of *Haunted Leadville* September 2025. Previous work includes *Sleeping Among Spirits (2022)*, *Unfinished Business (2023)*, *Unfinished Business #2 (2024)*, *Strange Colorado Volume 1 (2023)* and *Volume 2 (2024)*. Erin has been featured in *Shadow Zine*, Issue #6 with a focus on haunted Colorado Mining towns. When she's not writing, she has been out looking for ghosts, including hosting her cousin's American Hauntings ghost hunts in Colorado. Oh, and should probably include her family and pets are pretty awesome too.

## Adam White

Adam White, a native of a quaint Midwest town, discovered his fascination for the paranormal in his early years after an encounter with a phantom train. This initial spark ignited a lifelong passion that has driven him for over two decades. He has an extensive portfolio of hundreds of cases, articles in magazines and newspapers, and appearances on popular platforms like Coast-to-Coast AM and MTV. Beyond investigations, he has shared his knowledge through teaching workshops and community college courses on the subject. Additionally, for two decades, he has been a dedicated local tour guide for the Haunted Decatur Tours. He is also the host of the American Dread podcast.

## Troy Taylor

Troy Taylor is the author of more than 150 books on history, hauntings, true crime, the unexplained, and the supernatural in America. He is the founder of American Hauntings Ink, which offers books, events,

Illinois. He is also the writer and co-host of the American Hauntings Podcast. He has appeared in numerous television shows and documentaries, and his book about the St. Louis Exorcism of 1949 is currently under option to be turned into a film by a major production company.

and ghost tours, and is the owner of the American Oddities Museum in Alton,

www.ingramcontent.com/pod-product-compliance
Lightning Source LLC
Chambersburg PA
CBHW081643040426
42449CB00015B/3436